Grace
Abounding

To The Chief
Of Sinners

Grace
Abounding
To The Chief
Of Sinners

John Bunyan

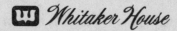 Whitaker House

Unless otherwise indicated, all Scripture quotations are taken from the *New King James Version* (NKJV), © 1979, 1980, 1982, 1984 by Thomas Nelson, Inc. Used by permission.

GRACE ABOUNDING

ISBN: 0-88368-259-1
Printed in the United States of America
Copyright © 1993 by Whitaker House

Whitaker House
30 Hunt Valley Circle
New Kensington, PA 15068

4 5 6 7 8 9 10 11 12 13 14 / 06 05 04 03 02 01 00 99 98

Chapter One

In this my recounting of the merciful working of God upon my soul, it will not be amiss if in the first place in a few words, I give you a hint of my pedigree and manner of upbringing, so that the goodness and bounty of God towards me may be all the more promoted and magnified before the sons of men.

About my ancestry then, it was, as is well known by many, of a low and inconsiderable generation; my father's house was of that class that is lowest and most despised of all the families in the land. Thus I have not here, as others could, boasted of noble blood, or of any highborn state according to the flesh; although, all things considered, I magnify the heavenly Majesty, for by this door he brought me into this world to partake of the grace and life that is in Christ by the gospel. But yet, notwithstanding the inferiority of my parents' humble position, it pleased God to put it into their hearts to send me to school to

3

learn both to read and write. These I also attained according to the rate of other men's children. However, to my shame I confess I did soon lose that little I learned, even almost completely, and that loss was long before the Lord did work his gracious work of conversion upon my soul.

As for my own natural life for the time that I was without God in the world, it was indeed *"according to the course of this world,"* and *"by nature children of wrath"* (Ephesians 2:2-3). It was my delight to be *"taken captive by the devil to do his will,"* (2 Timothy 2:26), being filled with all unrighteousness, which did also so strongly work and put forth itself both in my heart and life, that from a child I had few equals, especially considering my tender years, for cursing, swearing, lying, and blaspheming the holy name of God. Yes, so settled and rooted was I in these things that they became as a second nature to me, which, as I have also with soberness considered since, did so offend the Lord, that even in my childhood He did scare and frighten me with fearful dreams and did terrify me with fearful visions. For often, after I had spent the day in sin, I have in my bed been greatly afflicted while asleep with the apprehensions of devils and wicked spirits, who still, as I then thought, labored to draw me away with them, and of which I could never be rid.

Also, I would during these years be greatly afflicted and troubled with the thoughts of the fearful torments of hell-fire, still fearing that it would be my lot to be found at last among those devils and hellish fiends who are there bound down with the chains and bonds of darkness until the judgment of the great day. When I was but a child of nine or ten years old, these things did so distress my soul, that then, in the midst of my many sports and childish vanities, amid my vain companions, I was often much cast down and afflicted in my mind with them, yet could I not let go of my sins. I was also then so overcome with despair of life and heaven, that I would often wish either that there had been no hell, or that I had been a devil—supposing devils were only tormentors—that if it must be that I went there, I might be rather a tormentor than be tormented myself.

A while after those terrible dreams left me, and I soon forgot—for my pleasures did quickly cut off the remembrance of them, as if they never had been—then with more greediness, according to the strength of nature, I still let loose the reins of my lust and delighted in all transgressions against the law of God; so that until I came to the state of marriage, I was the very ringleader of all the youth that kept me company in all manner of vice and ungodliness. Yes, such control had the lusts and fruits of the flesh on this poor soul of mine that, had not a miracle of precious grace prevented, I would have not only perished by the stroke of eternal justice, but also laid myself open even to the stroke of those laws which bring some to disgrace and open shame before the face of the world.

In those days the thoughts of religion were very grievous to me. I could neither endure it myself nor that anyone else should, to the extent that when I saw some read in those books concerned with Christian piety, it would be, as it were, a prison to me. Then I said unto God, *"Depart from me, for I do not desire the knowledge of Your ways"* (Job 21:14). I was now void of all consideration. Heaven and hell were both out of sight and mind, and as for saving and damning, they were least in my

6

thoughts. Oh Lord, You know my life, and my ways were not hidden from You.

But this I well remember, that though I could myself sin with the greatest delight and ease and also take pleasure in the vileness of my companions, yet even then, if I had at any time seen wicked things in those who professed goodness, it would make my spirit tremble. One time stands out above all the rest. I was in the height of vanity, yet upon hearing one swear that was reckoned for a religious man, it had so great an impact upon my spirit that it made my heart ache.

God did not utterly leave me, but followed me still, not with convictions, but judgments, yet such were mixed with His mercy. Once I fell into a creek of the sea and hardly escaped drowning. Another time I fell out of a boat into the Bedford river, but mercy yet preserved me alive. Another time when I was in the field with one of my companions, it chanced that an adder passed over the highway. Having a stick in my hand, I struck her over the back, and having stunned her, I forced open her mouth with my stick and plucked her sting out with my fingers. By that act, had not God been merciful unto me, I might by my desperateness have brought myself to my end.

The following also I have taken notice of with thanksgiving. When I was a soldier, I with others was selected to go to such a place to besiege it. But when I was just ready to go, one of the company desired to go in my stead. When I had consented, he took my place. Coming to the siege, as he stood sentinel, he was shot in the head by a musket ball and died. Here as I said, were judgments and mercy, but neither of them did awaken my soul to righteousness. Therefore I sinned still, growing more and more rebellious against God and careless of my own salvation.

Chapter Two

Presently after this I changed my condition into a married state, and my mercy was to happen upon a wife whose father was counted godly. This woman and I, though we came together as poor as poor might be—not having so much household stuff as a dish or spoon between us both— yet this she had for her part, *The Plain Man's Pathway to Heaven* and *The Practice of Piety,* which her father had left her when he died. In these two books I would sometimes read with her, in which I found some things that were somewhat pleasing to me, but all the while I met with no conviction. She also would be often telling me what a godly man her father was, how he would reprove and correct vice both in his house and among his neighbors, and what a strict and holy life he lived in his days, both in words and deeds.

Thus these books, along with the relatives, though they did not reach my heart to awaken it about my sad and sinful state, yet they did begin within me some desires to reform my vicious life and fall in very eagerly with the religion of the times, specifically to go to church twice a day, attending with the most prominent religious men. There I would very devoutly both say and sing as others did, yet retaining my wicked life.

Nevertheless I was so overrun with the spirit of superstition, that I adored with greatest devotion all things—the high place, priest, clerk, vestment, service, and all else—belonging to the church. I counted all things holy that were therein contained. I especially considered the priest and clerk most happy and without doubt greatly blessed, because they were the servants of God and were principal in the holy temple to do His work there. This distortion grew so strong in a little time upon my spirit, that had I but seen a priest, though never so sordid and debauched in his life, I should find my spirit fall under him, reverence him, and knit unto him. Yes, thought I, for the love I did bear unto them, supposing they were the ministers of God, I could have laid down at their feet and been trampled upon by them—their name, their garments, and their work did so intoxicate and bewitch me.

After I had been thus for some considerable time, another thought came into my mind. That was whether we were of the Israelites or not. Finding in the Scriptures that they were once the peculiar people of God, I thought that if I were one of this race, my soul must be happy. Now again I found within me a great longing to be resolved about this question, but could not tell how I should. At last I asked my father about it, and he told me we were not. Wherefore then my spirit fell as to the hopes of that, and so remained downcast.

But all this while I was not sensible of the danger and evil of sin; I was kept from considering that sin would damn me, whatever religion I followed, unless I was found in Christ. No, I never thought of Him, nor whether there was such a one or not. Thus man, while blind, wanders, *"but the labor of fools wearies him, for he does not even know how to go to the city of God"* (Ecclesiastes 10:15).

But one day, among all the sermons our parson made, his subject was the treatment of the Sabbath day and of the evil of breaking that, either with labor, sports, or

11

otherwise. Now I was, notwithstanding my religion, one that took much delight in all manner of vice, and especially Sunday was the day that I comforted myself therewith. Wherefore I fell in my conscience under this sermon, thinking and believing that he made that sermon on purpose to show me my evil-doing. At that time I felt what guilt was, though never before that I can remember. However, I was for the present time greatly loaded with guilt, and so went home when the sermon was ended with a great burden upon my spirit.

This for that instant did numb the power of my best delights and embitter my former pleasures to me. But behold, it did not last, for before I had well dined, the trouble began to go out of my mind, and my heart returned to its old course. Oh, how glad was I that this trouble was gone from me and that the fire was put out, that I might sin again without control. Wherefore, when I had satisfied nature with my food, I shook the sermon out of my mind, and to my old custom of sports and gaming I returned with great delight.

But the same day, as I was in the middle of a game of cat, and having struck it one blow from the hole, just as I was about to strike it a second time, a voice suddenly darted from heaven into my soul, which said, "Will you leave your sins and go to heaven, or have your sins and go to hell?" At this I was exceedingly amazed.

Leaving my bat upon the ground, I looked up to heaven. It was as if I had, with the eyes of my understanding, seen the Lord Jesus looking down upon me, being very displeased with me and as if he severely threatened me with some grievous punishment for these and other ungodly practices. No sooner had I conceived this in my mind, than suddenly this conclusion was fastened on my spirit—for the former hint did set my sins again before my face—that I had been a great and grievous sinner, and that it was now too late for me to look toward heaven, for Christ would not forgive me nor pardon my transgressions.

Then I fell to musing on this also. While I was thinking of it and fearing that it should be so, I felt my heart sink in despair, concluding it was too late. Therefore I resolved in my mind to go on in sin, because I reasoned, if the case be thus, my state is surely miserable—miserable if I leave my sins and miserable if I follow them. I can but be damned; and if it must be so, I might as well be damned for many sins as be damned for few.

Thus I stood in the middle of my play before all that then were present, yet I told them nothing. But, having made this conclusion, I returned desperately to my sport again. I well remember that soon this kind of despair did so possess my soul that I was persuaded I could never attain to any other comfort than what I should get in sin, for heaven was gone already, so that on that I must not think. Wherefore I found within me a great desire to take my fill of sin, still studying what sin was yet to be committed, that I might taste the sweetness of it. I made as much haste as I could to fill my belly with its delicacies, lest I should die before I had sated my desires— for that I feared greatly.

In these things I proclaim before God that I do not lie, nor do I exaggerate this sort of speech. These were really, strongly, and with all my heart, my desires. May the good Lord, whose mercy is unsearchable, forgive my transgressions. I am very confident that this temptation of the devil is more usual among poor creatures than many are aware of, even to overrunning their spirits with a seared frame of heart and a numbing of conscience, the frame of which he quietly and slyly supplies with such despair that, though no peculiar guilt rests upon them, yet they continually have a secret conclusion within them that there is no hope for them because they have loved sins, and so after them they will go. (See Jeremiah 2:25 and 18:12.)

Now therefore I went on in sin with great greediness of mind, still grudging that I could not be satisfied with it as I would like. This continued with me about a month or more. But one day, as I was standing at a neighbor's shop window, cursing and swearing and playing the madman after my wanton manner, inside there sat the woman of the house, who heard me. Though she was a very loose and ungodly wretch, yet she protested that I swore and cursed at such a most fearful rate that she was made to tremble to hear me. She told me further that I was the ungodliest fellow for swearing that she ever heard in all her life, and that I, by thus doing, was able to spoil all the youth in the whole town if they but came in my company. At this reproof I was silenced and put to secret shame, and also, I thought, before the God of heaven. Wherefore while

I stood there hanging down my head, I wished with all my heart that I might be a little child again and that my father might teach me to speak without this wicked way of swearing. I reasoned that I was so accustomed to it that it was in vain for me to think of reformation, which I thought could never be.

But—how it came to pass I know not—from that time forward I did so quit my swearing that it was a great wonder to myself to observe it. Whereas before I did not know how to speak unless I put an oath before and another after to make my words have authority, now I could without an oath speak better and with more pleasantness than ever before. All this while I knew not Jesus Christ, neither did I stop my sports and plays.

But quickly after this I fell into company with one poor man that made a profession of religion, who, as I then thought, did talk pleasantly of the Scriptures and of the matter of religion. Falling into some love and liking with what he said, I took to my Bible and began to take great pleasure in reading, but especially the historical parts. As for Paul's epistles and such Scriptures, I could not understand them, being as yet ignorant of the corruption of our nature and of the need and worth of Jesus Christ to save us. Thus I fell to some outward reformation both in my words and life and set the commandments before me for my way to heaven, which commandments I also did strive to keep. As I thought I kept them pretty well sometimes, I would then have comfort. Yet now and then I would break one and so afflict my conscience, but I would repent and say I was sorry for it, promising God to do better next time. There I got help again, for then I thought I pleased God as well as any man in England.

In this manner I continued for about a year. All the time our neighbors took me to be a very godly man, a new and religious man, and marveled much to see such great and famous alteration in my life and actions. Indeed so it was, though I knew not Christ, nor grace, nor faith, nor hope. As I have well since seen, had I then died my state would have been most fearful. But, I say, my neighbors were amazed at my great conversion from prodigious profaneness to something like a moral life. Truly so they well might have been, for this my conversion was as great as for Tom of

Bedlam to become a sober man. Therefore they began to praise, to commend, and to speak well of me, both to my face and behind my back. Now I was, as they said, becoming godly—I was becoming a right honest man. When I understood those were their words and opinions of me, it pleased me very well, for though as yet I was nothing but a poor painted hypocrite, yet I loved to be talked of as one that was truly godly. I was proud of my godliness, and indeed I did all I did either to be seen or to be well spoken of by men. Thus I continued for about twelve months or more.

Chapter Three

Now you must know that before this, I had taken much delight in ringing the steeple bells. But with my conscience beginning to be tender, I thought such a practice was vain and therefore forced myself to stop it. Yet my mind yearned for it, so I would go to the church and watch, even though I dared not ring the bells. I thought this was not becoming to religion either, yet I forced myself and would look on still.

Soon after I began to consider what would happen if one of the bells should fall. Then I chose to stand under a main beam that overlay the church from side to side, thinking here I might stand safely. But then I thought if the bell should fall with a swing, it might first hit the wall, and rebounding upon me, might kill me because of this beam. This made me stand in the church door. Now, I thought I was safe enough, for if the bell should fall, I could slip out behind these thick walls and so be preserved. So after this I would yet go to see them ring, but would not go any further than the door. But then it came into my head, "What if the church steeple itself should collapse?" This thought—it may be for nothing I know when I stood and looked on—did continually so shake my mind that I dared not stand at the door any longer, but was forced to flee for fear the building would fall upon my head.

Another thing was my dancing: it was a full year before I could quite quit that. All this while, when I thought I kept this or that commandment, or did by word or deed anything I thought was good, I had great peace in my conscience and would think to myself, "God cannot but be now pleased with me." Yes, to relate it in my own way, I thought no man in England could please God better than I. But, poor wretch as I was, I was all this while ignorant of Jesus Christ, going about to establish my own righteousness, in which I would have perished had not God in mercy showed me more of my state by nature.

But one day the good providence of God called me to Bedford to work at my trade. In one of the streets of that town, I came where there were three or four poor women sitting at a door in the sun talking about the things of God. Being now willing to hear their discourse, I drew near to hear what they said, for I was now a brisk talker myself in the matters of religion. I will say I heard, but understood not, for they were far above my reach. Their talk was about a new birth, the work of God in their hearts, and also how they were convinced of their miserable state by nature. They talked how God had visited their souls with His love in the Lord Jesus, and with what words and promises they had been refreshed, comforted, and supported against the temptations of the devil. Moreover, they spoke about the suggestions and temptations of Satan in particular, and told each other by what means they had been afflicted, and how they were strengthened under his assaults. They also discoursed about their own wretchedness of heart and their unbelief, and did condemn, slight, and abhor their own righteousness as filthy and insufficient to do them any good.

I thought they spoke as if joy did make them speak. They talked with such pleasantness of scriptural language and with such appearance of grace in all they said, that they were to me as if they had found a new world—as if they were people that lived alone and were not to be regarded among their neighbors. At this I felt my own heart begin to shake and mistrust my condition to be nothing, for I saw that in all my thoughts about religion and salvation, the new birth never had entered my mind, neither knew I the comfort of the Word and promise, nor the deceitfulness and treachery of my own wicked heart. As for secret thoughts, I took no notice of them, neither did I understand what Satan's temptations were, nor how they were to be withstood and resisted.

Thus, when I had heard and considered what they said, I left them and went about my employment again, but their talk and conversation went with me. Also my heart stayed with them, for I was greatly affected by their words, both because by them I was convinced that I wanted the true tokens of a truly godly man, and also because by them I was convinced of the happy and blessed condition of him that was such a one. Therefore I would often make it my business to be going again and again into the company of these poor people, for I could not stay away. The more I went among them, the more I questioned my condition. As I still remember, presently I found two things within me at which I did sometimes marvel, especially considering what a blind, ignorant, sordid, and ungodly wretch I was. The one was a very great softness and tenderness of heart which caused me to fall under the conviction of what by Scripture they asserted; the other was a great bending in my mind to a continual meditating on it and on all other good things at any time I heard or read of them.

By these things my mind was now so fixated that it lay like a horse leech at the vein, still crying out, *"Give, give"* (Proverbs 30:15). My mind was so focused on eternity and on the things about the kingdom of heaven, that so far as I knew—though as yet God knows I knew but little—neither pleasures, nor profits, nor persuasions, nor threat could loosen it or make it let go of its hold. Although I may speak it with shame, yet it is indeed a certain truth that it would then have been as difficult for me to have taken my mind from heaven to earth as I have found it often since to get it again from earth to heaven.

One thing I may not omit. There was a young man in our town to whom my heart before had been knitted more than to any other, but as he was a most wicked creature for cursing and swearing and uncleanness, I now shook him off and forsook his company. About a quarter of a year after I had left him, I met him in a certain lane and asked him how he did. In his old swearing and mad way, he answered that he was well. "But, Harry," said I, "Why do you curse and swear so? What will become of you if you die in this condition?"

He answered me with great agitation, "What would the devil do for company if it were not for such as I am?"

About this time I came across some books written by ranters that were endorsed by some of our countrymen. These books were also held in high esteem by several old church members. Some of these I read but was unable to make any judgment about them. Therefore as I read them and considered their position, finding myself unable to judge, I would take myself to hearty prayer in this manner: "O Lord, I am a fool and not able to know the truth from error. Lord, leave me not to my own blindness, either to approve of or condemn this doctrine. If it be of God, let me not despise it; if it be of the devil, let me not

24

embrace it. Lord, I lay my soul in this matter only at Your feet. Let me not be deceived, I humbly ask You."

I had one religious companion all this while, and that was the poor man I spoke of before. But about this time he also turned a most devilish ranter and gave himself up to all manner of filthiness, especially uncleanness. He would also deny that there was a God, angel, or spirit, and would laugh at all exhortations to sobriety. When I labored to rebuke his wickedness, he would laugh more, purporting that he had gone through all religions and had never hit upon the right one until now. He told me also that in a little time I should see all professing Christians turn to the ways of the ranters. Wherefore, abominating those cursed principles, I left his company immediately and became to him as great a stranger as I had been before a friend.

Neither was this a temptation to just me. Because my work was located in the country, I happened to come into several people's company who, though formerly very devout in religion, yet were also drawn away by these ranters. These would talk with me of their ways and condemn me as legalistic and dark, professing that they had attained perfection, that they could do what they pleased and not sin. Oh, these temptations were suitable to my flesh, I being but a young man and my nature in its prime. But God, who had designed me for better things, kept me in the fear of His name and did not allow me to accept such cursed principles. Blessed be God, who put it into my heart to cry to Him to be kept and directed, still distrusting my own wisdom, for I have since seen even the effects of that prayer in His preserving me not only from ranting errors, but from those also that have sprung up since. The Bible was precious to me in those days.

Now I thought I began to look into the Bible with new eyes and read as I never did before. The epistles of the apostle Paul were especially sweet and pleasant to me. Indeed, I was never out of the Bible, either by reading or meditation, still crying out to God that I might know the truth and the way to heaven and glory. As I went on and read, I hit upon that passage, *"To one is given the word of wisdom through the Spirit; to another, the word of knowledge through the same Spirit; to another, faith...*" (1 Corinthians 12:8-9). Though I have since seen that by this Scripture the Holy Ghost intends in special things extraordinary, yet on me it did then fasten with conviction that I needed things ordinary, even that understanding and wisdom that other Christians had. On this word I mused and could not tell what to think. Especially the word *faith* put me to it, for I could not help but sometimes question whether I had any faith or not. I was loath to conclude I had no faith, for if I did so, I thought then I was counting myself a castaway indeed.

"No," said I to myself, "though I am convinced that I am an ignorant sot and that I want those blessed gifts of knowledge and understanding that other people have, yet I will conclude I am not altogether faithless, though I know not what faith is." For it was shown me—by Satan, as I have seen since—that those who conclude themselves in a faithless state have neither rest nor quiet in their souls, and I was loath to fall quite into despair.

By this suggestion I was for awhile made afraid to see my need of faith; but God would not allow me to undo and destroy my soul in such a way. Continually against my sad and blind conclusion, He created within me such suppositions that I could not rest content until I came to some certain knowledge as to whether I had faith or not. This debate was always running in my mind: "How can you tell if you lack faith indeed? But how can you tell if you have faith?" And besides, I saw for certain that if I did not have faith, I was sure to perish forever. Although I endeavored at the first to overlook the business of faith, yet shortly, having better considered the matter, I was willing to test myself as to whether I had faith or not. But alas, poor wretch, so ignorant and brutish was I, that I did not know how to do it any more than I knew how to begin and accomplish a rare and curious piece of art which I never yet saw or considered.

While I was considering and fretting about it—for you must know that as yet I had not in this matter revealed my mind to anyone else, only to listen and consider— the tempter came in with the delusion that there was no way for me to know I had faith but by trying to work some miracles, using those Scriptures that seem to appear that way for enforcing and strengthening his temptation.

One day as I was traveling between Elstow and Bedford, the temptation was strong to test if I had faith by doing a miracle, which at the time was this: I must say to the puddles that were in the horse pads, "Be dry," and to the dry places, "Be puddles." Truly one time I was going to say so indeed, but just as I was about to speak, the thought came into my mind, "First go behind that hedge and pray that God would make you able." When I had concluded praying, the idea came to me that since I had prayed, and if nothing happened when I tried to do it, then surely I had no faith and was a lost castaway. I thought, "If it be so, I will not try yet, but will stay a little longer." Thus I continued at a great loss, for I thought if only they which could do such wonderful things had faith, then I concluded that for the present I neither had it, nor yet for the time to come was ever likely to have it. So I was tossed between the devil and my own ignorance and was so perplexed, especially sometimes, that I could not tell what to do.

Chapter Four

About this time the happiness and state of these poor people at Bedford were presented to me in a kind of vision. I saw as if they were on the sunny side of some high mountain, refreshing themselves with the pleasant beams of the sun, while I was shivering and shrinking in the cold, afflicted with frost, snow, and dark clouds. I thought also between me and them I saw a wall that encompassed this mountain. Now through this wall my soul greatly desired to pass, concluding that if I could, I would even go into the very middle of them, and there also comfort myself with the heat of their sun. I saw myself going around this wall again and again, still prying as I went to see if I could find some way or passage by which I might enter, but none could I find for some time. At the last I saw a narrow gap, like a little doorway in the wall, through which I attempted to pass. Now the passage being very straight and narrow, I made many efforts to get in, but all in vain, even until I was quite exhausted by striving to enter. At last, with great effort, I thought I at first did get my head in, and after that, by a sidelong effort, my shoulders and my whole body. Then being exceeding glad, I went and sat down in the middle of them, and so was comforted with the light and heat of their sun.

Now the meanings of the mountain and wall were thus revealed to me. The mountain signified the church of the living God; the sun that shone there, the comfortable shining of His merciful face on those that were there; the wall was the wall that made the separation between Christians and the world; and the gap that was in the wall was Jesus Christ, who is the way to God the Father (John 14:6; Matthew 7:14). But as much as the passage was wonderfully narrow, even so narrow that I could not but with great difficulty enter in there, it showed me that none could enter into life but those that were in downright earnest, and unless also they left that wicked world behind them, for here was only room for body and soul, not for body and soul and sin. This sense abided in my spirit for many days, during which time I saw myself in a forlorn and sad condition. But yet I was provoked to a vehement hunger and desire to be one of that number that sat in the sunshine. Now also would I pray wherever I was, whether at home or away, in house or field. I would also often, with lifting up of heart, sing from the fifty-first Psalm, *"O Lord, consider my distress,"* for as yet I knew not where it was.

As yet I could not be certain to any comfortable degree that I had faith in Christ. Instead of having satisfaction here, I began to find my soul being assaulted with fresh doubts about my future happiness, especially with such thoughts as these: "Was I elected? But what if the day of grace should be past and gone?" By these two temptations I was very much afflicted and disquieted, sometimes by one and sometimes by the other.

First, to speak about my questioning my election, I found at this time that though I was very eager to find the way to heaven and glory, and though nothing could keep me from this, yet this question did so offend and discourage me that it was, especially sometimes, as if the very strength of my body had been taken away by the force and power thereof. Also this

Scripture seemed to me to trample upon all my desires: *"It is not of him that wills, nor of him that runs, but of God that shows mercy"* (Romans 9:16). With this Scripture I could not tell what to do, for I clearly saw that, unless God in His infinite grace and bounty had voluntarily chosen me to be a vessel of mercy, although I should desire and long and labor until my heart did break, it would be to no avail. Therefore these questions would stick with me: "How can you tell that you are elected? And what if you are not? What then?"

"O Lord," I cried, "what if I am not indeed?"

"Maybe you are not," said the tempter.

"It may be so indeed," thought I.

"Why then," said Satan, "you might as well stop now and strive no further; for if indeed you are not elected and chosen of God, there is no hope of your being saved, for *'it is not of him that wills, nor of him that runs, but of God that shows mercy.'"* By these things I was driven to my wits' end, not knowing what to say or how to answer these torments. Indeed, I little thought that Satan had thus assaulted me, but thought it was my own prudence thus to start the question. That the elect only obtained eternal life, I without scruple did heartily agree; but that I myself was one of them, there lay the question.

For several days I was greatly assaulted and perplexed, and was often, when I had been walking, ready to sink where I went from faintness of heart. But one day, after I had been for many weeks oppressed and cast down with this, as I was now quite giving up the ghost of all my hopes of ever attaining life, this sentence fell with weight upon my spirit: "Look at the generations of old and see if ever any trusted in God and yet were confounded."

With that I was greatly enlightened and encouraged, for at that very instant it was expounded to me: "Begin at the beginning of Genesis, and read to the end of the Revelation, and see if you can find that there was ever any that trusted in the Lord but was confounded." So coming home, I presently went to my Bible to see if I could find that saying, not doubting but to find it presently, for it was so fresh and with such strength and comfort to my spirit that it was as if it talked with me. Well, I looked but could not find it, yet it stayed with me.

Then I asked first one good man and then another, if they knew where it was located, but they knew of no such verse. At this I wondered that such a sentence should so suddenly and with such comfort and strength seize in my heart, and yet that none could find it, for I doubted not but that it was in the Holy Scriptures.

Thus I continued for more than a year but could not find the place. At last, casting my eye upon the Apocryphal books, I found it in Ecclesiasticus 2:10. This at the first did somewhat daunt me, but because by this time I had more experience of the love and kindness of God, it troubled me less, especially when I considered that though it was not in those texts that we call holy and canonical, yet as much as this sentence was the sum and substance of many of the promises, it was my duty to take comfort in it. I bless God for that word, for it was of good to me. That word does still many times shine before my face.

After this, another doubt did come with strength upon me, "What if the day of grace should be past and gone?" How do you know if you have overstayed the time of mercy? Now I remember that one day as I was walking in the country, I was much in thought about this, "But what if the day of grace is past?" To aggravate my trouble, the tempter presented to my mind those good people of Bedford and suggested to me that, these being converted already, they were all that God would save in those parts, and that I had come too late, for they had received the blessing before I came. Now I was in great distress, thinking indeed that this might well be so. Wherefore I went up and down bemoaning my sad condition, counting myself far worse than a thousand fools for standing off thus long, and spending so many years in sin as I had done, still crying out, "Oh, that I had turned sooner. Oh, that I had turned seven years ago." It made me angry with myself to think that I should have no more sense but to trifle away my time till my soul and heaven were lost.

But when I had been long vexed with this fear and was scarcely able to take one step more, just about the same place where I received my other encouragement, these words broke into my mind, *"And still there is room...Compel them to come in, that my house may be filled."* (Luke 14:22-23). These words, but especially those, *"and still there is room,"* were sweet words to me, for truly I thought that by them I saw there was place enough in heaven for me.

Moreover, when the Lord Jesus spoke these words, He then thought of me; and knowing that the time would come that I would be afflicted with fear that there was no place left for me in His bosom, He spoke this word and left it in the record that I might find help thereby against this vile torture. This I truly believed. In the light and encouragement of this word I went for some time. The comfort was even more when I thought that the Lord Jesus should consider me so long ago, and that He should speak those words on purpose for my sake, for I truly believed that He did on purpose speak them to encourage me.

But I was not without my temptations to go back again—temptations, I say, both from Satan, mine own heart, and carnal acquaintances—but I thank God they were outweighed by that sound sense of death and of the day of judgment which stayed continually in my view. I would often also think of Nebuchadnezzar, of whom it was said He had given him all the kingdoms of the earth (Daniel 5:18-19). Yet, thought I, if this great man had all his portion in this world, one hour in hell-fire would make him forget all. This consideration was a great help to me.

About this time I was made to see something concerning the beasts that Moses counted clean and unclean. Those beasts were types of men: the clean typified the people of God; but the unclean were types of such as were children of the wicked one. Now I read that the clean beasts chewed the cud: that is, they show us we must feed upon the Word of God. They also parted the hoof. I thought that signified we must part, if we would be saved, with the ways of ungodly men. In further reading about them, I also found that we are still unclean if we chew the cud as cattle does, but walk with claws like a dog; or, if we part the hoof like the swine, but do not chew the cud as the sheep. I thought the hare to be a type of those that talk of the Word yet walk in the ways of sin, and that the swine was like he that parts with his outward pollution but still lacks the word of faith, without which there would be no way of salvation, let a man be ever so devout (Deuteronomy 14).

After this I found, by reading the Word, that those that must be glorified with Christ in another world, must be called by Him here—called to the partaking of a share in His Word and righteousness, to the comforts and first fruits of His Spirit, and to a peculiar interest in all those heavenly things which do indeed prepare the soul for that rest and house of glory which is in heaven above.

Here again I was at a very uncomfortable spot, not knowing what to do, fearing I was not called. I thought that if I was not called, what then could do me good? None but those who are effectually called inherit the kingdom of heaven. But how I now loved those words that spoke of a Christian's calling, as when the Lord said to one, *"Follow me,"* and to another, *"Come after me."* Thought I, "Oh, that He would say so to me too; how gladly would I run after Him." I cannot now express with what longings and sighings in my soul I cried to Christ to call me. Thus I continued for a time all aflame to be converted to Jesus Christ, and did also see at that day such glory in a converted state that I could not be contented without a share therein. Gold! Could it have been purchased for gold, what I would have given for it! Had I had a whole world, it would have all gone ten thousand times over for this, that my soul might have been in a converted state. How lovely now was every one in my eyes that

I thought to be a converted man or woman. They shone; they walked like a people that carried the broad seal of heaven about them. Oh, I saw the lot was fallen to them in pleasant places and that they had a goodly heritage (Psalm 16:6).

But the verse which made me sick was that one about Christ, *"He went up into a mountain, and called to Him those He Himself wanted, and they came to Him"* (Mark 3:13). This Scripture made me faint and fear, yet it kindled a fire in my soul. That which made me fear was this: that Christ should have no liking for me, for He called whom He would. But the glory that I saw in that condition did still so engage my heart that I could seldom read of any that Christ did call, but that I presently wished, "Would that I had been in their place. Would that I had been born Peter. Would that I had been born John, or would that I had been by and heard Him when He called them." How I would have cried, "Oh, Lord, call me also." But I feared He would not call me.

And truly the Lord let me go on this way for many months altogether and showed me nothing—neither that I was already called, nor that I should be called hereafter. But at last, after much time spent and many groans to God that I might be made partaker of the holy and heavenly calling, that word came in upon me: *"I will acquit them of bloodguilt whom I had not acquitted; for the Lord dwells in Zion"* (Joel 3:21). These words, I thought, were sent to encourage me to wait still upon God, and signified unto me that if I were not already, yet the time might come when I might be in truth converted unto Christ.

About this time I began to share my mind to those poor people in Bedford and to tell them my condition. When they had heard, they told Mr. Gifford of me, who himself also took occasion to talk with me and was willing to be well persuaded of me, though, I think, from little grounds. But he invited me to his house, where I heard him confer with others about the dealings of God with their souls, from which I received more conviction. From that time I began to see something of the vanity and inward wretchedness of my wicked heart, for as yet I knew no great matter therein. Now it began to be discovered by me and also to work at a rate it never did before.

Now I evidently found that lusts and corruptions put forth themselves within me in wicked thoughts and desires, which I did not regard before. My desires also for heaven and life began to fail. I found also that, where before my soul was full of longing after God, now it began to yearn after every foolish vanity. Yes, my heart would not be moved to mind that which was good: it began to be careless both of my soul and heaven. It would now continually hang back, both to and in every duty, and was as a clog upon the leg of a bird to hinder him from flying. Thought I, "Now I grow worse and worse. I am further from conversion than ever I was before." Therefore I began to sink greatly in my soul and began to entertain such discouragement in my heart that it laid me as low as hell. If now I should have burned at the stake, I could not believe that Christ had a love for me. Alas, I could neither hear nor see Him, nor savor any of His things. I was driven as with a tempest; my heart would be unclean, and the Canaanites would dwell in the land.

Sometimes I would tell my condition to the people of God which, when they heard, they would pity me and would tell me of the promises. But they might as well have told me that I must reach the sun with my finger as to have bidden me receive or rely upon the promises, and as soon I should have done it. All my sense and feeling were against me, and I saw I had a heart that would sin and that lay under a law that would condemn. These things have often made me think of the child which the father brought to Christ, who, while he was yet coming to Him, was thrown down by the devil, so rent and tormented by him that he wallowed on the ground, foaming at the mouth (Mark 9:20, Luke 9:42).

Further, in these days I would find my heart shutting itself up against the Lord and against His Holy Word. I have found my unbelief to set as it were the shoulder to the door to keep Him out, even when I have with many a bitter sigh cried, "Good Lord, break it open. Lord, break these gates of brass, and cut these bars of iron asunder" (Psalm 107:16). Yet that word would sometimes create in my heart a peaceful pause, *I will gird you, though you have not known Me* (Isaiah 45:5). But all this while, as to the act of sinning, I was never more tender than now. I dared not take a pin or stick, though but so big as a straw, for my conscience now was sore and would smart at every touch. I could not

now tell how to speak, for fear I should
pervert my words. Oh, how cautiously did
I then go in all I did or said. I found myself
as in a miry bog, that shook if I did but
stir, and was as though left there both by
God and Christ and the Spirit, and all good
things.

But I observed, though I was such a
great sinner before conversion, yet God
never much charged the guilt of the sins of
my ignorance upon me. Rather He showed
me I was lost if I did not have Christ,
because I was a sinner. I saw that I lacked
a perfect righteousness to present me without fault before God, and this righteousness was nowhere to be found but in the
person of Jesus Christ. But my original and
inward pollution was my plague and affliction: this I saw at a dreadful rate always
putting forth itself within me, and I had
the guilt of this to my amazement. By
reason of that, I was more loathsome in my
own eyes than a toad and thought I was so
in God's eyes, too. Sin and corruption
would as naturally bubble out of my heart
as water would bubble out of a fountain. I
thought now that every one had a better
heart than I had. I could have exchanged
hearts with anybody. I thought none but

the devil himself could equal me for inward wickedness and pollution of mind. Therefore, at the sight of my own vileness, I fell deeply into despair. I concluded that this condition that I was in could not stand with a state of grace. Thought I, "Surely I am forsaken of God. Surely I am given up to the devil and to a reprobate mind." Thus I continued for a long while, even for some years altogether.

While I was thus afflicted with the fears of my own damnation, there were two things that would make me wonder. The one was, when I saw old people hunting after the things of this life as if they should live here always. The other was, when I found believers much distressed and cast down when they met with outward losses, as of husband, wife, or child. "Lord," I thought, "What ado is here about such little things as these. What seeking after carnal things by some, and what grief in others for the loss of them. If they so much labor after and shed so many tears for the things of this present life, how I am to be bemoaned, pitied, and prayed for. My soul is dying, my soul is damned. Were my soul but in a good condition, and were I but sure of it, how rich should I esteem myself, though blessed but with bread and water. I should count those but small afflictions and should bear them as little burdens. *'Who can bear a broken spirit?'* (Proverbs 18:14)."

And though I was much troubled and tossed and afflicted with the sight and sense and terror of my own wickedness, yet I was afraid to let this sight and sense go quite from my mind. I found that unless guilt of conscience was taken care of the right way—that is, by the blood of Christ— a man grew rather worse from the loss of his peace of mind than before. Therefore, when my guilt rested hard upon me, then I would cry that the blood of Christ might take it. If guilt was lessening without the blood—for the sense of sin would be sometimes as if it would fade and go quite away—then I would also strive to bring it upon my heart again by directing the punishment of sin in hell-fire upon my spirit and would cry, "Lord, let it not leave my heart but in the right way, by the blood of Christ and the application of Your mercy through Him to my soul." That Scripture did stay much in my mind, *"Without shedding of blood there is no remission"* (Hebrews 9:22). What made me even more afraid of this was because I had seen some who, when they were under the wounds of conscience, would cry and pray. Yet when they felt an easing of their troubled spirits rather than a pardon for their sins, they cared not how they lost their guilt, so they put it out of their minds. Now, having it removed the wrong way, it was not sanctified unto them, so they grew harder and blinder and more wicked after their trouble. This made me afraid and made me cry to God all the more that it might not be so with me.

And now I was sorry that God had made me a man, for I feared I was a reprobate. I counted unconverted man as the most doleful of all creatures. Thus being afflicted and tossed about in my sad condition, I counted myself alone and above the most of men unblessed. Yes, I thought it impossible that I should ever attain to so much godliness of heart as to thank God that he had made me a man. Man indeed is the most noble by creation of all creatures in the visible world, but by sin he has made himself the most ignoble. The beasts, birds, fishes—I have blessed their condition, for they had not a sinful nature. They were not obnoxious to the wrath of God;

they were not to go to hell-fire after death. I could therefore have rejoiced had my condition been as any of theirs.

Chapter Five

I existed in this condition for a great while, but when the comforting time came, I heard someone preach a sermon on these words in the Song, *"Behold, you are fair, my love! behold, you are fair"* (Song of Solomon 4:1). But at that time he made these two words, *"my love,"* his chief subject matter, from which, after he had a introduced the text, he drew these several conclusions:

- The church, and so every saved soul, is Christ's love even when loveless.
- Christ's love is without a cause.
- Christ's love has been hated by the world.
- Christ's love continues when under temptation and desertion.
- Christ's love is from first to last.

I got nothing from what he said at that time, except when he came to the application of the fourth point, this was what he said: "If it be so that the saved soul is Christ's love even when under temptation and desertion, then, poor tempted soul, when you are assaulted and afflicted with temptations and the hiding of His face, yet think on these two words, '*my love*,' still."

So as I was coming home, these words came again into my thoughts. I well remember, as they came, I said thus in my heart, "What shall I get by thinking on these two words?" This thought had no sooner passed through my heart than these words began thus to kindle in my spirit, "You are My love, you are My love," some twenty times together. Still as they ran through my mind they grew stronger and warmer, and began to make me look up. But being as yet between hope and fear, I still replied in my heart, "But is it true? Is it true?" To which, that sentence fell upon me, *"He did not know that what was done by the angel was real"* (Acts 12:9).

Then I began to give place to the word, which with power did over and over make this joyful sound within my soul, "You are My love, you are My love, and nothing shall separate you from My love." And with that my heart was filled full of comfort and hope, and now I could believe that my sins would be forgiven me. Yes, I was now so taken with the love and mercy of God, that

I remember I could not tell how to contain myself till I got home. I thought I could have spoken of His love and have told of His mercy to me, even to the very crows that sat upon the plowed lands before me, had they been capable of understanding me. Therefore I said in my soul with much gladness, "Well, if I had a pen and ink here, I would write this down before I go any further, for surely I shall not forget this forty years from now." But alas, within less than forty days I began to question it all again, which made me begin to question all still.

Yet at times I was helped to believe that it was a true manifestation of grace unto my soul, though I had lost much of the life and savor of it. Now about a week or two after this, I was much hounded by this Scripture: *"Simon, Simon, indeed Satan has asked for you, that he may sift you as wheat"* (Luke 22:31). Sometimes it would sound so loud within me and, as it were, call so strongly after me, that once above all the rest I turned my head over my shoulder, thinking truly that some man behind me had called me. Being at a great distance, I thought he had called so loudly that it came, as I have thought since, to stir me up to prayer and to watchfulness. It came to inform me that a cloud and a storm were coming down upon me, but I understood it not. Also, as I remember, the time that it called to me so clearly was the last time that it sounded in my ears. But I think I still hear with what a loud voice these words *"Simon, Simon"* sounded in my ears. I was certain, as I have told you, that somebody had called after me that was half a mile behind me. Although that was not my name, yet it made me suddenly look behind me, believing that he that called so noisily meant me.

But so foolish and ignorant was I that I knew not the reason of this sound, which, as I did both see and feel soon after, was sent from heaven as an alarm to awaken me to provide for what was coming. However, I would muse and wonder in my mind what the reason of this Scripture was, and that at this rate so often and so clearly it should still be sounding and ringing in my ears. But, as I said before, I soon after perceived the purpose of God therein. About the space of a month later, a very great storm came down upon me, which handled me twenty times worse than all I had met with before. It came stealing upon me, now by one piece and then by another. First, all my comfort was taken from me; then darkness seized upon me; after which whole floods of blasphemies, both against God, Christ, and the Scriptures, were poured upon my spirit, to my great confusion and astonishment.

These blasphemous thoughts were such as stirred up questions in me against the very being of God and of His only beloved Son, as to whether there was in truth a God or Christ, and whether the Holy Scriptures were not a fable and cunning story rather than the holy and pure Word of God. The tempter would also assault me often with this, "How can you tell but that the Turks had Scriptures equally as good to prove their Muhammad the Savior as we have to prove our Jesus? And, how could I think that so many tens of thousands in so many countries and kingdoms should be without the knowledge of the right way to heaven, if there were indeed a heaven, and that we only, who live in a corner of the earth, should alone be blessed therewith? Everyone does think his own religion is the most right, Jews and Moors and pagans. What if all our faith and Christ and Scriptures should be but a 'think so' too?"

Sometimes I endeavored to argue against these suggestions and to set some of the sentences of blessed Paul against them. But alas, I quickly felt, when I thus did, such arguings as these would return again to assail me: "Though we made so great a matter of Paul and of his words, yet how can I tell but that in very deed he, being a subtle and cunning man, might give himself up to deceive with strong delusions, and also take the pains and travail to undo and destroy his fellows?"

These suggestions, with many others which at this time I may not and dare not utter by word or pen, made a very great seizure upon my spirit. They did so overweigh my heart both with their number, continuance, and fiery force, that I felt as if there were nothing else but these from morning to night within me, and as though indeed there could be room for nothing else. I also concluded that God had, in wrath to my soul, given me up to them, to be carried away with them as with a mighty whirlwind. Only by the distaste they gave to my spirit did I feel there was something in me that refused to embrace them. But this consideration I then only had when God allowed me to swallow my spittle, otherwise the noise and strength and force of these tortures would drown, overflow, and bury all such thoughts or the remembrance of any such thing.

While I was in this torment, I often found in my mind a sudden urge to curse and swear, or to speak some grievous thing against God, Christ His Son, or of the Scriptures. Now I thought, surely I am possessed of the devil. At other times, I thought I should be bereft of my senses; for instead of praising and magnifying God the Lord with others, if I but heard Him spoken of, presently some most horrible blasphemous thought or other would bolt out of my heart against Him. So whether I did think that God was, or again did think there was no such thing as God, no love, peace, or gracious disposition could I feel within me.

These things did sink me into very deep despair, for I concluded that such things could not possibly be found among them that loved God. Often when these temptations had been with force upon me, I compared myself to the case of a child whom some gypsy had by force taken up in her arms and was carrying from friend and country. Kick sometimes I did, and also shriek and cry, but yet I was bound in the wings of the temptation, and the wind would carry me away. I thought also of Saul and of the evil spirit that did possess him, and did greatly fear that my condition was the same as his (1 Samuel 16:14).

In these days, when I have heard others talk of what the sin against the Holy Ghost was, then the tempter would so provoke me to desire to sin that particular sin that it was as if I could not, must not, neither should be quiet until I had committed it. Now no sin would serve but that one. If it were to be committed by the speaking of such a word, then it was as if my mouth would have spoken that word, whether I would or not. In so strong a measure was this temptation upon me, that often I have been ready to clap my hands under my chin to hold my mouth from opening. To that end also I have had thoughts at other times to leap with my head downward into some muck hole or other to keep my mouth from speaking.

Now, again, I beheld the condition of the dog and toad, and counted the state of everything that God had made far better than this dreadful state of mine and my companions. Yes, gladly would I have been in the condition of a dog or horse, for I knew they had no soul to perish under the everlasting weight of hell or sin as mine was likely to do. Even though I saw this, felt this, and was broken to pieces with it, yet added to my sorrow was the knowledge that I could not find that with all my soul I desired deliverance. This Scripture did also tear and rend my soul in the middle of these distractions: *"The wicked are like the troubled sea, when it cannot rest, whose waters cast up mire and dirt. 'There is no peace,' says my God, 'for the wicked'"* (Isaiah 57:20-21).

And now my heart was at times exceedingly hard. If I would have given a thousand pounds for a tear, I could not shed one, nor sometimes scarcely desire to shed one. I was much dejected to think that this should be my lot. I saw some could mourn and lament their sin, and others could rejoice and bless God for Christ, and still others could quietly talk of and with gladness remember the Word of God, while I only was in the storm or tempest. This much sunk me. I thought my condition was alone. I would therefore much bewail my hard fortune, but get out of or get rid of these things I could not.

While this torture lasted, which was about a year, I could attend to none of the ordinances of God but with sore and great affliction; then I was most distressed with blasphemies. If I had been hearing the word, then uncleanness, blasphemies, and despair would hold me a captive there. If I was reading, then sometimes I had sudden thoughts to question all I read. At other times my mind would be so strangely snatched away and possessed with other things that I have neither known, nor regarded, nor remembered so much as the sentence that but now I had read.

In prayer also I was greatly troubled at this time. Sometimes I thought I felt Satan behind me pull my clothes. He would be also continually at me in time of prayer to quit. "Break off. Make haste. You have prayed enough, and stay no longer," still drew my mind away. Sometimes also he would cast in such wicked thoughts as these: that I must pray to him or for him. I have thought sometimes of that text, *"If you will fall down and worship me"* (Matthew 4:9). Also when, because I have had wandering thoughts in the time of this duty, I have labored to compose my mind and fix it upon God, then with great force the tempter labored to distract and confound me, and to turn away my mind by presenting to my heart and fancy the form of a bush, a bull, a broom, or the like, as if I should pray to these. To these he would also, at some times especially, so hold my mind, that I could think of nothing else, or pray to nothing else but to these or such as they.

Yet at times I would have some strong and heart-affecting apprehensions of God and the reality of the truth of His Gospel. How would my heart at such times put forth itself with inexpressible groanings! My whole soul was then in every word. I would cry with pangs after God, that he would be merciful unto me. But then I would be daunted again with such conceits as thinking that God mocked at these my prayers, saying in the audience of the holy angels, "This poor simple wretch hankers after me, as if I had nothing to do with my mercy but to bestow it on such as he. Alas, poor soul, how are you deceived. It is not for such as you to have favor with the Highest."

Then had the tempter come upon me also with such discouragements as these: "You are very hot for mercy, but I will cool you; this frame shall not last always. Many have been as hot as you for a time, but I have quenched their zeal." With this, someone who was fallen away would be set before my eyes. Then I would be afraid that I should do so too. Thought I, "But I am glad this comes into my mind. Well, I will watch, and take what care I can."

"Though you do," said Satan, "I shall be too hard for you. I will cool you insensibly by degrees, little and little. What care I," said he, "though I be seven years in chilling your heart, if I can do it at last? Continual rocking will lull a crying child asleep. I will ply it close, but I will have my end accomplished. Though you be burning hot at present, I can pull you from this fire. I shall have you cold before long."

These things brought me into great straits. At present I could not find myself fit for present death, so I thought to live longer would make me yet more unfit, because time would make me forget all and remove out of mind and thought even the remembrance of the evil of sin, the worth of heaven, and the need I had of the blood of Christ to wash me. But I thank Christ Jesus, these things did not at present make me slacken my crying, but rather did put me more upon it, like she who met with the adulterer (Deuteronomy 22:27). This was a good word to me in these days, after I had suffered these things awhile: *"I am persuaded that neither death, nor life, nor angels...shall be able to separate us from the love of God, which is in Christ Jesus"* (Romans 8:38-39). And now I hoped long life would not destroy me nor make me miss heaven.

I had some supports in this temptation, though they were then all questioned by me. That in Jeremiah 3:1 was something to me; and so was the consideration of verse four of that chapter, that though we have spoken and done as evil things as we could, yet we shall cry unto God, *"My Father, You are the guide of my youth,"* and shall return unto Him. I had also once a sweet glance from 2 Corinthians 5:21, *"For He made Him who knew no sin to be sin for us, that we might become the righteousness of God in Him."* I remember one day, as I was sitting in a neighbor's house, very sad at the consideration of my many blasphemies, I was saying in my mind, "What ground have I to think that I, who have been so vile and abominable, should ever inherit eternal life?" The verse came suddenly upon me, *"What then shall we say to these things? If God is for us, who can be against us?"* (Romans 8:31). Also John 14:19 was a help unto me, *"Because I live, you will live also."* These words were but hints, touches, and short visits, though very sweet when present, only they lasted not, but like Peter's sheet, suddenly were caught up from me to heaven again (Acts 10:16).

Afterwards the Lord did more fully and graciously reveal Himself unto me, and indeed did not only deliver me from the guilt that by these things was laid upon my conscience, but also from the very filth thereof. The temptation was removed, and I was put into my right mind again, as other Christians were. I remember that one day, as I was traveling into the country and musing on the wickedness and blasphemy of my heart, and considering the enmity that was in me to God, that Scripture came into my mind, *"Having made peace through the blood of His cross"* (Colossians 1:20). By this I was made to see, both again and again, that God and my soul were friends by His blood. Yes, I saw that the justice of God and my sinful soul could embrace and kiss each other, through His blood. This was a good day to me; I hope I shall never forget it.

At another time, as I sat by the fire in my house and was musing on my wretchedness, the Lord made this also a precious word unto me, *"Inasmuch then as the children have partaken of flesh and blood, He Himself likewise shared in the same, that through death He might destroy him who had the power of death, that is, the devil, and release those who through fear of death were all their lifetime subject to bondage"* (Hebrews 2:14-15). I thought that the glory of these words was then so weighty on me, that I was once or twice ready to faint as I sat, yet not with grief and trouble, but with solid joy and peace.

Chapter Six

A t this time also I sat under the ministry of holy Mr. Gifford, whose doctrine, by God's grace, was good for my stability. This man made it his business to deliver the people of God from all those hard and unsound tests that by nature we are prone to. He would bid us take special heed not to take any truth upon faith, from this source or that, or any other man or men, but rather we should cry mightily to God that He would convince us of the reality thereof and establish us therein by his own Spirit in the Holy Word. Said Mr. Gifford, "If you do otherwise, when temptation comes strongly upon you, you—not having received the Word with evidence from heaven—will find you lack that help and strength now to resist, that once you thought you had."

This was as timely to my soul as the former and latter rain in their season, for I had found, and that by sad experience, the truth of these his words. I had felt that *no man can say,* especially when tempted by the devil, *"that Jesus is Lord, except by the Holy Spirit"* (1 Corinthians 12:3). Wherefore I found my soul through grace very apt to drink in this doctrine and to incline to pray to God that, in nothing that pertained to God's glory and my own eternal happiness, He would suffer me to be without the confirmation thereof from heaven. Now I saw clearly that there was an exceeding difference between the notion of the flesh and the revelation of God in heaven. Also there was a great difference between the faith that is feigned according to man's wisdom and that which comes by revelation from God into a man's spirit (Matthew 16:17; 1 John 5:1).

But how my spirit was now led from truth to truth by God, even from the birth and cradle of the Son of God, to his ascension and second coming from heaven to judge the world. Truly I then found upon this account the great God was very good unto me, for to my remembrance there was not anything that I then cried unto God to make known and reveal unto me, but that He was pleased to do it for me—I mean, not one part of the Gospel of the Lord Jesus existed, but I was orderly led into it.

I thought I saw, with great evidence from the four evangelists, the wonderful works of God in giving Jesus Christ to save us, from His conception and birth even to His second coming to judgment. It was as if I had seen Him born, as if I had seen Him grow up, as if I had seen Him walk through this world from the cradle to the cross. I saw how gently He gave Himself to be crucified and nailed on the cross for my sins and wicked doings. As I was musing on His progress, that passage dropped into my spirit, *"He was foreordained for the slaughter"* (1 Peter 1:11, 20). When I considered the truth of His resurrection and remembered that word, *"Do not cling to me, Mary"* (John 20:17), I saw it was as if He had leaped out of the grave's mouth for joy that He was risen again and had obtained the conquest over our dreadful foes. I have also in the spirit seen Him sitting on the right hand of God the Father for me, and the manner of His coming from heaven to judge the world with glory, and have confirmed these things by these Scriptures: Acts 1:9, 7:56, 10:42; Hebrews 7:24; Revelation 1:18; and 1 Thessalonians 4:17-18.

Once I was troubled to know whether the Lord Jesus was man as well as God, and God as well as man. Truly in those days, let men say what they would, unless I had it with evidence from heaven, all was nothing to me, and I counted myself not set in any truth of God. I was very troubled about this point and could not tell how to resolve it. At last Revelation 5:6 came into my mind, *"And I looked, and behold, in the midst of the throne and of the four living creatures, and in the midst of the elders, stood a Lamb."* "In the middle of the throne," thought I, "there is the Godhead; in the middle of the elders, there is manhood." I thought this glistened. It was a good touch and gave me sweet satisfaction.

Another Scripture also that helped me much in this, *"For unto us a Child is born, unto us a Son is given: and the government will be upon His shoulder: and His name shall be called Wonderful, Counsellor, Mighty God, Everlasting Father, Prince of Peace"* (Isaiah 9:6). Also, besides these teachings of God in His Word, the Lord made use of two things to confirm me in this truth: the one was the errors of the fanatics, and the other was the guilt of sin. As the fanatics opposed the truth, so God all the more confirmed me in it by leading me into the Scriptures that wonderfully upheld it.

The errors the fanatics maintained were:

1. That the Holy Scriptures were not the Word of God.
2. That every man in the world had the Spirit of Christ, grace, faith, and so on.
3. That Christ Jesus, as crucified and dying sixteen hundred years ago, did not satisfy divine justice for the sins of the people now.
4. That Christ's flesh and blood were within the saints.
5. That the bodies of the good and bad that are buried in the churchyard shall not rise again.
6. That the resurrection has already passed for good men.
7. That that man Jesus who was crucified between two thieves on mount Calvary in the land of Canaan by Judea, did not ascend above the starry heaven.
8. That He should not, even the same Jesus that died by the hands of the Jews, come again at the last day, and as man judge all nations.

Many more vile and abominable things were in those days fomented by them, by which I was driven to a more thorough search of the Scriptures, and was, through their light and testimony, not only enlightened, but greatly confirmed and comforted in the truth.

As I said, the guilt of sin did help me much. Still, as that would come upon me, the blood of Christ did take it again and again, and that so sweetly, according to the Scriptures. Oh, friends, cry to God to reveal Jesus Christ unto you; there is none that teaches like Him.

It would be too long here to stay to tell you in particular how God did confirm me in all the things of Christ; and how He did, that He might do so, lead me into His words; and also how He did open them unto me, make them shine before me, and cause them to dwell with me, talk with me, and comfort me over and over, both of His own being and the being of His Son and Spirit, and Word and Gospel. Only this, as I said before and will say unto you again, that in general He was pleased to take this course with me: first to suffer me to be afflicted with temptations concerning them, and then reveal them unto me. Sometimes I would lie under great guilt for sin, even crushed to the ground with the weight of it, and then the Lord would show me the death of Christ. Yes, He so sprinkled my conscience with His blood that I would find, even before I was aware, that in this conscience, where but just now did reign and rage the law, even there would rest and abide the peace and love of God through Christ.

Now I had evidence, as I thought, of my salvation from heaven, with many golden seals thereon, all hanging in my sight. Now could I remember this manifestation and the other discovery of grace with comfort, and would often long and desire that the last day would come, that I might be forever inflamed with the sight and joy and communion with Him whose head was crowned with thorns, whose face was spit upon, whose body was broken, and whose soul was made an offering for my sins. Whereas before I lay continually trembling at the mouth of hell, now I thought I was so far from there that when I looked back I could scarce discern it. Thought I, "Oh, that I were eighty years old now, that I might die quickly, that my soul might be gone to rest."

But before I was very far away from these my temptations, I did greatly long to see some ancient godly man's experience, who had written some hundreds of years before I was born. Those who had written in our days—I thought, but I desire them now to pardon me—had written only that which others felt, or else had, through the strength of their intelligence, studied to answer such objections as they perceived others were perplexed with, without going down themselves into the deep.

Well, after many such longings in my mind, the God in whose hands are all our days and ways, did cast into my hands one day a book of Martin Luther's. It was his *Comment on the Galatians*. Also, the book was so old that it was ready to fall apart, if I did but turn it over. Now I was very pleased that such an old book had fallen into my hands. When I had perused but a little of it, I found my condition in his experience so largely and profoundly handled, as if his book had been written from my heart. This made me marvel, for thus thought I, "This man could not know anything of the state of Christians now, but had to write and speak about the experience of former days. Besides, he did most gravely also in that book debate about the rise of these temptations and torments—namely, blasphemy, desperation, and the like—showing that the law of Moses, as well as the devil, death, and hell, had a very great hand therein. At first this was very strange to me, but considering and watching, I found it to be so indeed. But of the particulars here I intend nothing, only this I think I must let be known before all men: I prefer this book of Martin Luther on the Galatians, excepting the Holy Bible, to all the books that ever I have seen, as most fit for a wounded conscience.

Now I found, as I thought, that I loved Christ dearly. Oh, I thought my soul clung unto Him, my affections held unto Him. I felt my love for Him was as hot as fire; and now, as Job said, I thought I should die in my nest. But I quickly found that my great love was but little, and that I, who had, as I thought, such burning love for Jesus Christ, could let him go again for a very trifle. God knows how to abase us and will not hide pride from a man.

Quickly after this my love was tried for a purpose. After the Lord had in this manner graciously delivered me from this great and sore torment, had established me so sweetly in the faith of His Holy Gospel, and had given me such strong consolation and blessed evidence from heaven touching my interest in His love through Christ, the tempter came upon me again, with a more grievous and dreadful temptation than before. That was, to sell and part with this most blessed Christ—to exchange Him for the things of this life, for anything. The temptation lay upon me for the space of a year and followed me so continually that I was not rid of it even for one day a month; no, sometimes not one hour in many days together, unless I was asleep, and though in my judgment I was persuaded that those who were once effectually in Christ, as I hoped through His grace I had seen myself, could never lose Him forever, for *"the land shall not be sold permanently; for the land is mine,' says God"* (Leviticus 25:23). Yet it was a continual vexation to me to think that I could have so much as one thought within me against Christ Jesus who had done for me as He had done; nonetheless then I had almost nothing but blasphemous thoughts.

Neither my dislike of the thoughts nor any desire and endeavor to resist them, did in the least shake or abate the continuation or force and strength thereof. It did always, in almost whatever I thought, intermix itself in such a way that I could neither eat my food, stoop for a pin, chop a stick, or cast my eyes to look on this or that, but still the temptation would come, "Sell Christ for this, or sell Christ for that; sell Him, sell Him." Sometimes it would run through my thoughts perhaps a hundred times altogether, "Sell Him, sell Him, sell Him." Against this for whole hours I have been forced to stand as continually leaning and forcing my spirit against it, unless unfortunately before I was aware, some wicked thought might arise in my heart that might consent thereto. Sometimes the tempter would make me believe I had consented to it. Then I would be as if tortured upon a rack for whole days at a time.

This temptation did bring me such fear that I would at some time consent to it and be overcome by it, that by the very force of my mind in laboring to resist this wickedness, my very body would be put in action or motion, by way of pushing or thrusting with my hands or elbows, still answering as fast as the destroyer said, "Sell him," "I will not, I will not, I will not. No, not for thousands and thousands of worlds." Thus I reckoned, for fear that I would in the middle of these assaults set too low a value on him, even when I scarcely knew where

I was or how to be composed again. At these seasons he would not let me eat my food in quiet; but, when I was sitting at the dinner table, I had to go hence to pray. I had to leave my food immediately, so counterfeitly holy would this devil be. When I was thus tempted, I would say in myself, "Now I am at dinner, let me make an end."

"No," said he, "you must do it now, or you will displease God and despise Christ." Thus I was much afflicted with these things, because of the sinfulness of my nature. If, imagining that these were impulses from God, I should deny to do it, would it not be as if I denied God? Then should I not be as guilty, because I did obey a temptation of the devil, as if I had broken the law of God indeed?

But to be brief, one morning as I lay in my bed I was, as at other times, most fiercely assaulted with this temptation to sell and part with Christ, the wicked suggestion still running in my mind, "Sell him, sell him, sell him, sell him," as fast as a man could speak. Against this also in my mind, as at other times, I answered, "No, no, not for thousands, thousands, thousands," at least twenty times together. At last, after much striving, even until I was almost out of breath, I felt this thought pass through my heart, "Let Him go if He will." I thought also that I felt my heart freely consent to this. Oh, the diligence of Satan! Oh, the desperateness of man's heart!

Now was the battle won, and down fell I, as a bird that is shot from the top of a tree, into great guilt and fearful despair. Thus getting out of my bed, I went moping into the fields—with as heavy a heart as mortal man I think could bear—where for the space of two hours I was like a man bereft of life, now past all recovery, and bound over to eternal punishment.

And that Scripture did seize upon my soul: *"Lest there be any...profane person like Esau, who for one morsel of food sold his birthright. For you know that afterward, when he wanted to inherit the blessing, he was rejected, for he found no place for repentance, though he sought it diligently with tears"* (Hebrews 12:16-17).

Now was I as one bound; I felt myself shut up into the judgment to come. Nothing for the next two years would abide with me but damnation and an expectation of damnation. I repeat, nothing now would abide with me but this—save some few moments for relief—as in the following you will see. These words were to my soul like fetters of brass to my legs, in the continual sound of which I went for several months. But about ten or eleven o'clock on that day, as I was walking under a hedge, full of sorrow and guilt, bemoaning myself for this hard fortune that such a thought should have arisen within me, suddenly this sentence rushed in upon me: "The blood of Christ remits all guilt." At this I made a stand in my spirit. With that this word took hold upon me, *"The blood of Jesus Christ His Son cleanses us from all sin"* (1 John 1:7).

Now I began to conceive peace in my soul. I thought it was as if the tempter did leer and steal away from me, as being ashamed of what he had done. At the same time also I had my sin and the blood of Christ thus represented to me: that my sin, when compared to the blood of Christ, was no more to it than this little clod or stone before me is to this vast and wide field that here I see. This gave me good encouragement for the space of two or three hours. During that time also I thought I saw by faith the Son of God suffering for my sins. Because it did not remain with me, I sunk in my spirit under exceeding guilt again, but chiefly by the aforementioned Scripture concerning Esau's selling of his birthright. That Scripture would lie all day long in my mind and hold me down, so that I could by no means lift up myself. When I would strive to turn to this Scripture or that for relief, still that sentence would be sounding in me: *"For you know that afterward, when he wanted to inherit the blessing, he found no place for repentance, though he sought it diligently with tears."* Sometimes, indeed, I would have a touch from Luke 22:32: *"I have prayed for you, that your faith should not fail."* But it would not stay with me; neither could I indeed, when I considered my state, find grounds to conceive in the least that there should be the root of that grace in me, having sinned as I had done. Now was I torn and rent in a heavy way for many days.

Then began I, with sad and careful heart, to consider the nature and largeness of my sin and to search into the Word of God, if I could in any place find a word of promise or any encouraging sentence by which I might take relief. Wherefore I began to consider Mark 3:28, *"All sins will be forgiven the sons of men, and whatever blasphemies they may utter."* I thought at a blush that this reference did contain a large and glorious promise for the pardon of high offenses. But considering the text more fully, I thought it was rather to be understood as relating chiefly to those who had, while in a natural state, committed such things as there are mentioned, but not to me, who not only had received light and mercy, but who had, both after and also contrary to that, so slighted Christ as I had done.

I feared therefore that this wicked sin of mine might be that sin unpardonable of which he there thus speaks, *"But he who blasphemes against the Holy Spirit never has forgiveness, but is subject to eternal condemnation"* (Mark 3:29). I did rather give credit to this, because of the sentence, *"For you know that afterward, when he wanted to inherit the blessing, he was rejected; for he found no place for repentance, though he sought it diligently with tears"* (Hebrews 12:17). This stuck always with me. Now was I both a burden and a terror to myself; I did ever so know now what it was to be weary of my life and yet afraid to die. Oh, how gladly I would have been anybody but myself, anything but a man, and in any condition but my own. There was nothing that did cross my mind more frequently than that it was impossible for me to be forgiven my transgression and be saved from the wrath to come.

Now I began to labor to recall times past, wishing a thousand times over that the day was yet to come when I should be tempted to such a sin, concluding with great indignation, both against my heart and all assaults, how I would rather be torn in pieces than be found a consenter to it. But, alas, these thoughts and wishes and resolutions were now too late to help me. The thought had passed my heart. God had let me go, and I was fallen. *"Oh, that I were as in months past, as in the days when God watched over me"* (Job 29:2).

Then again, being loath and unwilling to perish, I began to compare my sin with others, to see if I could find that any of those that were saved had done as I had done. So I considered David's adultery and murder, and found them most heinous crimes. Those too were committed after light and grace had been received. But yet, I considered that his transgressions were only such as were against the law of Moses, from which the Lord Christ could, with the consent of His Word, deliver him. But mine was against the Gospel and against the Mediator thereof: I had sold my Savior. Again I would be as if racked upon the wheel, when I considered that besides the guilt that possessed me, I should be so devoid of grace, so bewitched. I thought, "Must it be no sin but this? Must it have been the great transgression (Psalm 19:13)? Must that wicked one touch my soul (1 John 5:18)?" Oh, what sting did I find in all these sentences!

Further I thought, "Is there but one sin that is unpardonable, but one sin that lays the soul outside the reach of God's mercy? Must I be guilty of that— must it be that? Is there but one sin, among so many millions of sins, for which there is no forgiveness, and must I have committed this? Oh, unhappy sin! Oh, unhappy man!" These things would so break and confound my spirit, that I could not tell what to do. I thought at times they would have broken my sanity. Still to aggravate my misery, that would run in my mind, *"You know that afterward, when he wanted to inherit the blessing, he was rejected."* Oh, no one knows the terrors of those days but myself.

Chapter Seven

After this I began to consider Peter's sin, which he committed in denying his Master. Indeed this came nearest to mine of any that I could find, for he had denied his Savior as had I, after light and mercy had been received, and moreover after warning had been given him. I also considered that he did it once and twice, and that after time to consider between. But though I put all these circumstances together, that, if possible I might find help, yet I considered again that his was but a denial of his Master, but mine was a selling of my Savior. Wherefore I thought with myself that I came nearer to Judas than either to David or Peter. Here again, my torment would flame out and afflict me. Yes, it would grind me as it were to powder, to consider the preservation of God towards others while I fell into the snare. In my thus considering other men's sins and comparing them with my own, I could evidently see that God preserved them, notwithstanding their wickedness, and would not let them, as he had let me, become a son of perdition.

Oh, how my soul did at this time prize the preservation that God did set about His people. Ah, how safely did I see them walk whom God had hedged in. They were within his care, protection, and special providence: though they were fully as bad as I by nature, yet because He loved them, He would not suffer them to fall outside the range of mercy. But as for me, I was gone; I had done it; He would not preserve me nor keep me, but allowed me, because I was a reprobate, to fall as I had done. Now did those blessed places that speak of God's keeping His people shine like the sun before me, though not to comfort me, but to show me the blessed state and heritage of those whom the Lord had blessed.

Now I saw that as God had His hand in all the providences and dispensations that overtook His elect, so He had His hand in all the temptations that they had to sin against Him, not to spur them to wickedness, but to choose their temptations and troubles for them, and also to leave them for a time to such things only as might not destroy them, but rather humble them, and not put them beyond, but lay them in the way of the renewing of His mercy. Oh, what love, what care, what kindness and mercy did I now see mixing itself with the most severe and dreadful of all God's ways to His people. He would let David, Hezekiah, Solomon, Peter, and others fall, but He would not let them fall into the sin unpardonable, nor into hell for sin. Oh, thought I, these are the men that God had loved; these are the men that God, though He chastises them, keeps in safety by Him, and whom He makes to abide under the shadow of the Almighty.

But all these thoughts added sorrow, grief, and horror to me, as I now thought it was killing to me. If I thought how God kept His own, that was killing to me; if I thought of how I was fallen myself, that was killing to me. As all things work together for the best, and to do good to them that were the called according to His purpose (Romans 8:28), so I thought that all things worked for damage and for my eternal overthrow. Then, again, I began to compare my sin with the sin of Judas, that if possible I might find if mine differed from that which in truth is unpardonable. Thought I, "If it should differ from it, even though but the breadth of a hair, what a happy condition is my soul in." By considering I found that Judas did his intentionally, but mine was against prayer and striving. Besides, his was committed with deliberation, but mine in a fearful hurry suddenly. All this while I was tossed to and fro like the locust, and driven from trouble to sorrow, hearing always the sound of Esau's fall in mine ears, and the dreadful consequences thereof.

This consideration about Judas' sin was for awhile some little relief to me, for I saw I had not, as to the circumstances, transgressed as fully as he. But this was quickly gone again, for I thought to myself there might be more ways than one to commit this unpardonable sin. Also I thought there might be degrees of that as well as of other transgressions. Wherefore, this iniquity of mine might be such as might never be passed by, for nothing I yet could perceive. I was often now ashamed that I should be like such an ugly man as Judas. I thought also how loathsome I would be to all the saints in the day of judgment, to such an extent that now I could scarcely see a good man whom I believed had a good conscience, but I would feel my heart tremble at him while I was in his presence. Oh, now I saw a glory in walking with God, and what a mercy it was to have a good conscience before Him.

About this time, I was much tempted to content myself by receiving some false opinions, such as that there would be no such thing as a day of judgment; that we would not rise again; and that sin was no such grievous thing. The tempter suggested thus: "If these things should indeed be true, yet to believe otherwise would yield you ease for the present. If you must perish, never torment yourself so much beforehand. Drive the thoughts of damning out of your mind by possessing your mind with some conclusions that atheists and ranters use to help themselves."

When such thoughts fled through my heart, following right behind were how death and judgment have been in my view. I thought the Judge stood at the door. I felt as if it had come already, so that such things could have no entertainment. But I know now that Satan will use any means to keep the soul from Christ. He loves not an awakened frame of spirit. Security, blindness, darkness, and error are the very kingdom and habitation of the wicked one.

I found it a hard work now to pray to God, because despair was swallowing me up. I thought a tempest was driving me away from God, for always when I cried to God for mercy this would come in: "It is too late. I am lost. God has let me fall, not to my correction but my condemnation. My sin is unpardonable, and I know concerning Esau, how that, after he had sold his birthright, he would have received the blessing, but was rejected."

About this time I did light on that dreadful story of that miserable mortal, Francis Spira, a book that was to my troubled spirit as salt when rubbed into a fresh wound. Every sentence in that book, every groan of that man, with all the rest of his actions in his distress, as his tears, his prayers, his gnashing of teeth, his wringing of hands, his twisting and languishing and pining away under that mighty hand of God that was upon him, were as knives and daggers in my soul. Especially that sentence of his was frightful to me, "Man knows the beginning of sin, but who bounds the issues thereof?" Then would the former sentence, as the conclusion of all, fall like a hot thunderbolt again upon my conscience, *"For you know that afterward, when he wanted to inherit the blessing, he was rejected, for he found no place for repentance, though he sought it diligently with tears."*

Then would I be struck into a very great trembling, insomuch that at some times I could, for whole days, feel my very body as well as my mind shake and totter under the sense of this dreadful judgment of God that would fall on those that have sinned that most fearful and unpardonable sin. I felt also such a clogging and heat at my stomach, by reason of my terror, that I felt, especially at some times, as if my breastbone would split asunder. Then I thought concerning that of Judas, who by his falling headlong burst asunder, and all his bowels gushed out (Acts 1:18). I feared also that this was the mark that God did set on Cain, even continual fear and trembling, under the heavy load of guilt that He had charged on him for the blood of his brother Abel.

Thus did I twist and shrink under the burden that was upon me, which burden so oppressed me that I could neither stand nor go, nor lie either at rest or quiet. Yet that saying would sometimes come into my mind, *"You have received gifts among men, even for the rebellious*" (Psalm 68:18). Thought I, "The rebellious, why, surely they are such as once were under subjection to their Prince; even those who, after they have once sworn subjection to His government, have taken up arms against Him. And this is my very condition. I once loved Him, feared Him, served Him; but now I am a rebel. I have sold Him: I have said, 'Let Him go if He will.' But yet He has gifts for rebels; then why not for me?" This sometimes I thought about, and would labor hard to take hold of, that some small refreshment might have been conceived by me. But in this also I lacked desire; I was driven with force beyond it. I was like a man going to execution even by that place where he could happily creep in and hide himself, but may not.

Again, after I had thus considered the sins of the saints in particular, and found mine went beyond them, then I began to think to myself, "Set the case as I should, put all theirs together, and mine alone against them, might I not then find encouragement? For if mine, though bigger than any one of theirs, yet should it be but equal to all, then there is hope. For that blood that had virtue enough in it to wash away all of theirs, waould have virtue enough in it to wash away mine, though this one be fully as big, if not bigger than all theirs combined." Again, I would consider the sin of David, of Solomon, of Manasseh, of Peter, and the rest of the great offenders, and would also labor, where I might with fairness, to aggravate and heighten their sins by several circumstances. I would think to myself that David shed blood to cover his adultery, and that murder by the sword of the children of Ammon—a work that could not be done but by contrivance, which was a great aggravation to his sin.

But then this would turn upon me: "Ah, but these were but sins against the law, from which there was a Jesus sent to save them. But yours is a sin against the Savior, and who shall save you from that?"

Then I thought on Solomon, and how he sinned in loving strange women, in falling away to their idols, in building them temples, in doing this after light, in his old age, after he had received great mercy. But the same conclusion that cut me off in the former consideration, cut me off as to this—namely, that all these were but sins against the law, for which God had provided a remedy. But I had sold my Savior, and there remained no more sacrifice for sin. I would then add to these men's sins the sins of Manasseh, how he built altars for idols in the house of the Lord; he also observed times, used enchantments, had dealings with wizards, was a wizard, had his familiar spirits, burned his children in sacrifice to devils, and made the streets of Jerusalem run with the blood of innocents. I considered these to be great sins, sins of a bloody color. But yet it would turn again upon me, "None of them are of the nature of yours, for you have parted with Jesus: you have sold your Savior." This one consideration would always kill my heart—my sin was point-blank against my Savior, and at such a height that I had in my heart said of Him, "Let Him go if He will." Oh, I thought this sin was bigger than the sins of a country, of a kingdom, or of the whole world. No one pardonable sin, nor all of them together was able to equal mine; mine outdid them every one.

Now I would find my mind fleeing from God as from the face of a dreadful judge. Yet this was my torment, and I could not escape His hand, *It is a fearful thing to fall into the hands of the living God*" (Hebrews 10:31). But blessed be His grace, that Scripture in these flying fits would call, as if running after me: *"I have blotted out, like a thick cloud, your transgressions, and like a cloud, your sins: return to Me; for I have redeemed you"* (Isaiah 44:22). This, I say, would come in upon my mind when I was fleeing from the face of God. I did flee from His face—that is, my mind and spirit fled before Him, by reason of His highness that I could not endure. Then would the text cry, *"Return to Me."* It would cry aloud with a very great voice, *"Return to Me; for I have redeemed you."*

Indeed, this would make me pause a little and, as it were, look over my shoulder behind me to see if I could discern that the God of grace did follow me with a pardon in His hand. I could no sooner do that than all would be clouded and darkened again by that sentence: *"For you know that afterward, when he wanted to inherit the blessing, he found no place for repentance, though he sought it diligently with tears."* Wherefore I could not stop myself, but fled, though at sometimes it cried, *"Return, return,"* as if it followed after me. But I feared to come close lest the voice should not be from God, and because that other was still sounding in my conscience: *"For you know that afterward, when he wanted to inherit the blessing, he was rejected."*

Once, as I was walking to and fro in a good man's shop, bemoaning my end in my sad and doleful state, afflicting myself with self-abhorrence for this wicked and ungodly thought, lamenting also this hard lot of mine that I should have committed so great a sin, greatly fearing that I should not be pardoned, praying also in my heart that the Lord would show me if this sin of mine did differ from that against the Holy Ghost, and being now ready to sink with fear, suddenly there was as if there had rushed in at the window the noise of wind upon me, very pleasant, and as if I heard a voice speaking, "Did you ever refuse to be justified by the blood of Christ?" With that, my whole life of past profession was in a moment opened unto me, where I was made to see that designedly I had not. So my heart answered a groaning, "No."

Then fell with power that word of God upon me, *"See that you do not refuse Him who speaks"* (Hebrews 12:25). This made a strange seizure upon my spirit: it brought light with it and commanded a silence in my heart of all those tumultuous thoughts that before, like masterless hell-hounds, used to roar and bellow and make hideous noises within me. It showed me also that Jesus Christ had yet a word of grace and mercy for me—that He had not, as I had feared, quite forsaken and cast off my soul. Yes, this was a kind of check for my proneness to desperation—a kind of threatening of me, if I did not, notwithstanding my sins and the heinousness of them, venture my salvation upon the Son of God.

But as to my determining about this strange dispensation, what it was I know not, or from where it came I know not. I have not yet in twenty years' time since been able to make a judgment of it. I thought then what I should be loath here to speak. But truly that sudden rushing wind was as if an angel had come upon me. Both it and the salvation I will leave until the day of judgment. Only this I say: it commanded a great calm in my soul; it persuaded me there might be hope; it showed me, as I thought, what the sin unpardonable was, and that my soul had yet the blessed privilege to flee to Jesus Christ for mercy. But I say, concerning this dispensation, I know not yet what to say of it, which was also in truth the cause that at first I did not speak of it in the book. I do now also leave it to be thought about by men of sound judgment. I lay not the stress of my salvation thereupon, but upon the Lord Jesus in the promise. Yet seeing I am here unfolding my secret things, I thought it might not be altogether inexpedient to let this also show itself, though I cannot now relate the matter as then I did experience it. The savor of it lasted for about three or four days, and then I began to mistrust and to despair again.

Therefore still my life hung in doubt before me, not knowing which way I should go. Only this I found my soul desire, even to cast itself at the foot of grace by prayer and supplication. But it was shameful for me now to have to face this Christ, against whom I had thus vilely sinned. to pray for mercy. It was hard work, I say, to offer to look Him in the face against whom I had so vilely sinned, and indeed I have found it as difficult to come to God by prayer, after backsliding from Him, as to do any other thing. Oh, the shame that did now attend me, especially when I thought that I was now going to pray to Him for mercy that I had so lightly esteemed but a while before. I was ashamed, even confounded, because this villainy had been committed by me.

But I saw that there was only one way for me: I must go to Him, humble myself to Him, and beg that He of His wonderful mercy would show pity to me and have mercy upon my wretched sinful soul. When the tempter perceived this, he strongly suggested to me, "You ought not to pray to God, for prayer is not for any in your case; neither could it do you any good, because you had rejected the Mediator, by whom all prayers came with acceptance to God the Father, and without whom no prayer could come into His presence. Wherefore now to pray is but to add sin to sin. Yes, now to pray, seeing God has cast you off, is the next way to anger and offend Him more than you ever did before. For God has been weary of you for these several years already, because you are none of His. Your bawling in His ears has been no pleasant voice to Him, and therefore He let you sin this sin, that you might be quite cut off. Will you pray still?"

This the devil urged, and set forth that in Numbers, when Moses said to the children of Israel that because they would not go up to possess the land when God would have them, thus forever He did bar them out from there, though they prayed that they might with tears. As it is said in another place, *"But if a man acts with premeditation against his neighbor...you shall take him from My altar, that he may die"* (Exodus 21:14), even as Joab was by king Solomon, when he thought to find shelter there (1 Kings 2:28-34). These verses did pinch me very sorely. Yet, my case being desperate, I thought to myself, I can but die. If it must be so, it shall once be said that such a one died at the foot of Christ in prayer. This I did, but with great difficulty, God knows, because with this still that saying about Esau would be set at my heart, even like a flaming sword, to keep the way of the tree of life, for fear that I should take of it and live.

Oh, who knows how hard a thing I found it to come to God in prayer. I did also desire the prayers of the people of God for me, but I feared that God would give them no heart to do it. Yes, I trembled in my soul to think that some or other of them would shortly tell me that God had said those words to them that He once did say to the prophet concerning the children of Israel: *"'Do not pray for this people, for I will not hear them'* (Jeremiah 11:14), so pray not for him, for I have rejected him."

Yes, I thought that He had whispered this to some of them already, only they dared not tell me so. Neither dared I ask them of it, for fear, if it should be so, it would make me quite beside myself. "Man knows the beginning of sin," said Spira, "but who bounds the issues thereof?"

About this time I took an opportunity to express my mind to a mature, wise Christian and told him all my case. I told him that I was afraid that I had sinned the sin against the Holy Ghost, and he told me he thought so too. Here therefore I had but cold comfort, but talking a little more with him, I found him, though a good man, a stranger to much combat with the devil. Therefore I went to God again, as well as I could, for mercy still. Now also did the tempter begin to mock me in my misery, saying that, seeing I had thus parted with the Lord Jesus and provoked Him to displeasure who would have stood between my soul and the flame of devouring fire, there was now but one way, and that was to pray that God the Father would be a mediator between His Son and me, that He would be reconciled again, and that I might have that blessed benefit in Him that His saints enjoyed. Then did that Scripture seize upon my soul: *"He is unique, and who can make Him change?"* (Job 23:13). Oh, I saw it was as easy to persuade Him to make a new covenant or a new Bible besides those we have already, as to pray for such a thing. This was to persuade Him that what He had done already was mere folly and persuade him to alter, yes, to disannul the whole way of salvation. Then would that saying rend my soul asunder, *"Nor is there salvation in any other, for there is no other name under heaven given among men, by which we must be saved"* (Acts 4:12).

Now the most free and full and gracious words of the Gospel were the greatest torment to me. Yes, nothing so afflicted me as the thought of Jesus Christ. The remembrance of a Savior, because I had cast Him off, brought forth the villainy of my sin and my loss by it to mind. Nothing did twinge my conscience like this. Everything that I thought of the Lord Jesus, of His grace, love, goodness, kindness, gentleness, meekness, death, blood, promises and blessed exhortations, comforts and consolations, went to my soul like a sword. Still unto my considerations of the Lord Jesus, these thoughts would make place for themselves in my heart: "Aye, this is the Jesus, the loving Savior, the Son of God whom you have parted with, whom you have slighted, despised, and abused. This is the only Savior, the only Redeemer, the only one that could so love sinners as to wash them from their sins in His own most precious blood, but you have no part nor lot in this Jesus. You have put Him from you. You have said in your heart, 'Let Him go if He will.' Now therefore you are severed from Him. You have severed yourself from Him. Behold then His goodness, but yourself to be no partaker of it."

"Oh, what I have lost! What I have parted with! What has disinherited my poor soul! How sad to be destroyed by the grace and mercy of God—to have the Lamb, the Savior, turn lion and destroyer," I wailed. I also trembled at the sight of the saints of God, especially those who greatly loved Him and who made it their business to walk continually with Him in this world, for they did in their words, their carriage, and all their expressions of tenderness and fear to sin against their precious Savior, condemn, lay guilt upon, and add continual affliction and shame unto my soul. The dread of them was upon me, and I trembled at God's Samuel (1 Samuel 16).

Chapter Eight

Now the tempter began afresh to mock my soul another way, saying that Christ indeed did pity my case and was sorry for my loss, but since I had sinned and transgressed as I had done, He could by no means help me nor save me from what I feared. My sin was not of the nature of theirs for whom He bled and died, neither was it counted with those that were laid to His charge when He hung on the tree. Therefore, unless He should come down from heaven and die anew for this sin, though indeed He did greatly pity me, yet I could have no benefit of Him.

These things may seem ridiculous to others—even as ridiculous as they were in themselves—but to me they were most tormenting cogitations. Every one of them augmented my misery, that Jesus Christ should have so much love as to pity me when yet He could not help me too. Neither did I think that the reason why He could not help me was because His merits were weak, or His grace and salvation spent on others already, but because His faithfulness to His threatenings would not let Him extend His mercy to me. Besides, as I have already hinted, I thought that my sin was not within the bounds of that pardon that was wrapped up in a promise; and if not, then I knew surely that it was more easy for heaven and earth to pass away than for me to have eternal life. So the ground of all these fears of mine did arise from a steadfast belief I had of the stability of the holy Word of God and also from my being misinformed of the nature of my sin. But how this added to my affliction, to conceive that I should be guilty of such a sin for which He did not die! These thoughts did so confound and imprison me, and bind me up from faith, that I knew not what to do.

Thought I, "Oh, that He would come down again! Oh, that the work of man's redemption was yet to be done by Christ." How I prayed to Him and entreated Him to count and reckon this sin among the rest for which He died. But this Scripture would strike me down as dead, *"Christ having been raised from the dead, dies no more. Death no longer has dominion over Him"* (Romans 6:9). Thus by the strange and unusual assaults of the tempter, my soul was like a broken vessel, driven as with the winds and tossed sometimes headlong into despair—sometimes upon the covenant of works, and sometimes to wish that the new covenant and the conditions thereof might, so far as I thought myself concerned, be turned another way and changed. But in all these I was as those that jostle against the rocks—more broken, scattered, and torn.

Oh, the previously unconceived imaginations, frights, fears, and terrors that are effected by a thorough application of guilt yielding to desperation! This is as the man that has his dwelling among the tombs with the dead, who is always crying out and cutting himself with stones (Mark 5:2-5). But, I say, all in vain: desperation will not comfort him, the old covenant will not save him. No, heaven and earth shall pass away before one jot or title of the Word and law of grace will fail or be removed. This I saw, this I felt, and under this I groaned. Yet this advantage I got thereby, namely, a further confirmation of the certainty of the way of salvation, and that the Scriptures were the Word of God. Oh, I cannot now express what I then saw and felt of the steadiness of Jesus Christ, the rock of man's salvation. What was done could not be undone, added to, or altered. I saw indeed that sin might drive the soul beyond Christ, even the sin which is unpardonable. But woe to him that was so driven, for the Word would shut him out.

Thus was I always sinking, whatever I did think or do. So one day I walked to a neighboring town, sat down upon a settee in the street, and fell into a very deep pause about the most fearful state my sin had brought me to. After long musing, I lifted up my head, but what I thought I saw was as if the sun that shines in the heavens did grudge to give light, and as if the very stones in the street and tiles upon the houses did bend themselves against me. I thought that they all combined together to banish me out of the world. I was abhorred of them, and unfit to dwell among them, or be partaker of their benefits, because I had sinned against the Savior. Oh, how happy now was every creature to what I was, for they stood fast and kept their station, but I was gone and lost.

Then crying out in the bitterness of my soul, I said to my soul with a grievous sigh, "How can God comfort such a wretch?" I had no sooner said it but this returned upon me as an echo answers a voice, "This sin is not unto death." At that, it was as if I had been raised out of the grave and cried out again, "Lord, how could You find out such a word as this?" I was filled with admiration at the fitness and at the unexpectedness of the sentence—the fitness of the word, the rightness of the timing of it. The power and sweetness and light and glory that came with it were marvelous to me to find.

I was now, for the time, out of doubt as to that about which I was so much in doubt before. My fears before were that my sin was not pardonable, and so I had no right to pray and to repent; or if I did, it would be of no advantage or profit to me. But now I thought that if this sin is not unto death, then it is pardonable. Therefore from this I have encouragement to come to God by Christ for mercy and to consider the promise of forgiveness as that which stands with open arms to receive me as well as others.

This idea greatly eased my mind, that my sin was pardonable, that it was not the sin unto death (1 John 5:16-17). None but those that know what my trouble was from their own experience, can tell what relief came to my soul by this consideration. It was a release to me from my former bonds, and a shelter from my former storms. I seemed now to stand on the same ground with other sinners, and to have as much right to the Word and prayer as any of them.

Now, I say, I was in hopes that my sin was not unpardonable, but that there might be hope for me to obtain forgiveness. But how Satan did now lay about to bring me down again! But he could by no means do it, neither that day nor the most part of the next, for that sentence, "This sin is not unto death," stood like a mill post at my back. Yet towards the evening of the following day, I felt this word begin to leave me and to withdraw its support from me.

So I returned to my old fears again, but with a great deal of grudging and peevishness, for I feared the sorrow of despair. My faith could not long retain this word. But the next evening, being under many fears, I went to seek the Lord. As I prayed, I cried, and my soul cried to Him in these words with strong cries: "Oh Lord, I beseech You, show me that You have loved me with an everlasting love." I had no sooner said it than with sweetness this came back to me as an echo resounding: *"I have loved you with an everlasting love"* (Jeremiah 31:3). Now I went to bed in quiet. When I awoke the next morning, it was fresh on my soul, and I believed it.

But yet the tempter left me not, for it could not be so little as a hundred times that he that day did labor to break my peace. Oh, the combats and conflicts that I did then meet with. As I strove to hold to this word, that about Esau would fly in my face like lightning. I would be sometimes up and down twenty times in an hour. Yet God did bear me out and keep my heart upon this passage, from which I had also for several days obtained very much sweetness and comfortable hopes of pardon. Thus it was made unto me: "I loved you while you were committing this sin. I loved you before, I love you still, and I will love you forever."

Yet I saw my sin most barbarous and a filthy crime, and could not but conclude, with great shame and astonishment, that I had horribly abused the holy Son of God. Therefore I felt my heart greatly love and pity Him and my soul yearn for Him, because I saw He was still my friend and did reward me good for evil. Yes, the love and affection that then did burn within me for my Lord and Savior, Jesus Christ, did work at this time a strong and earnest desire of revenge upon myself. For the abuse I had done unto Him, to speak as I then thought, had I a thousand gallons of blood within my veins, I could freely then have spilled it all at the command and feet of this my Lord and Savior.

As I was thus musing, and in my studies considering how to love the Lord and to express my love to Him, that saying came to me: *"If You, Lord, should mark iniquities, O Lord, who could stand? But there is forgiveness with You, that You may be feared"* (Psalm 130:3-4). These were good words to me, especially the latter part, that there is forgiveness with the Lord, that He might be feared. That is, as I then understood it, that He might be loved and held in reverence. It was thus shown to me that the great God did set so high an esteem upon the love of His poor creatures, that rather than going without their love, He would pardon their transgressions. Now was this word fulfilled in me, and I was also refreshed by it, *"That you may remember and be ashamed, and never open your mouth any more because of your shame,*

*when I provide you an atonement for all
you have done, says the Lord God"* (Ezekiel
16:63).

Thus was my soul at this time, and as
I then did think, forever set at liberty from
being afflicted with my former guilt and
amazement. But before many weeks were
gone I began to despond again, fearing
that, notwithstanding all I had enjoyed, I
might be deserted and destroyed at the
last. This consideration came strong into
my mind: that whatever comfort and peace
I thought I might have from the Word of
the promise of life, yet unless there could
be found in my refreshment a concurrence
and agreement with the Scriptures—let me
think what I will thereof and hold it ever
so fast—I should find no such thing at the
end, for the Scripture cannot be broken
(John 10:35). Now began my heart again to
ache and fear I might meet with disap-
pointment at the last. Wherefore I began
with all seriousness to examine my former
comfort, and to consider whether one that
had sinned as I had done might with confidence trust upon the faithfulness of God
laid down in these words by which I had
been comforted, and on which I had leaned
myself.

But now was brought to my mind, *"For it is impossible for those who were once enlightened, and have tasted of the heavenly gift, and have become partakers of the Holy Spirit, and have tasted the good word of God and the powers of the age to come, if they fall away, to renew them again to repentance"* (Hebrews 6:4-6). *"For if we sin willfully after we have received the knowledge of the truth, there no longer remains a sacrifice for sins, but a certain fearful expectation of judgment and fiery indignation, which will devour the adversaries"* (Hebrews 10:26-27). *"Like Esau, who for one morsel of food sold his birthright. For you know that afterwards, when he wanted to inherit the blessing, he was rejected, for he found no place for repentance, though he sought it diligently with tears"* (Hebrews 12:17).

Now was the word of the Gospel forced from my soul, so that no promise or encouragement was to be found in the Bible for me. Now would that saying work upon my spirit to afflict me, *"Do not rejoice, O Israel, for joy like other peoples"* (Hosea 9:1). I saw indeed there was cause of rejoicing for those that held to Jesus, but for me, I had cut myself off by my transgressions and left

114

myself neither foothold nor handhold among all the stays and props in the precious Word of life.

Truly I now felt myself sink into a gulf, as a house whose foundation is destroyed. I likened myself in this condition to the case of a child that had fallen into a pit, who, though able to make some attempts to scramble and sprawl in the water, yet because he could find no solid hold, at last it must die in that condition.

As soon as this fresh assault had fastened on my soul, that Scripture came into my heart. *"This for many days."* Indeed I found it was so, for I could not be delivered nor brought to peace again until two-and-a-half years were completely finished. Wherefore these words, though in themselves they tended to no discouragement, yet to me, who feared this condition would be eternal, they were at some times as a help and a refreshment to me. I reassured myself with the thought that many days are not forever—many days will have an end. Therefore, seeing I was to be afflicted not a few, but many days, yet I was glad it was but for many days. This, I say, I would recall for myself sometimes and give myself a help. As soon as ever the word came into my mind, at first I knew my trouble would be long. Yet this would be but sometimes, for I could not always think on this, nor even be helped by it, though I did.

Now while the Scriptures lay before me and laid sin anew at my door, that saying in Luke 18:1, with others, did encourage me to pray. Then the tempter again assailed me very sorely, suggesting that neither the mercy of God nor yet the blood of Christ did at all concern me, nor could they help me for my sin. Therefore it was but in vain to pray. "Yet," thought I, "I will pray."

"But," said the tempter, "your sin is unpardonable."

"Well," said I, "I will pray."

"It is for no good," said he.

"Yet," said I, "I will pray."

So I went to prayer to God. While I was at prayer, I uttered words to this effect: "Lord, Satan tells me that neither Your mercy nor Christ's blood is sufficient to save my soul. Lord, shall I honor You most by believing You will and can, or him, by believing You neither will nor can? Lord, I would honor You by believing You will and can." And as I was thus before the Lord, that Scripture fastened on my heart, "O *man, great is your faith,"* even as if one had clapped me on the back as I was on my knees before God. Yet I was not able to believe that this was a prayer of faith, till almost six months after, for I could not think that I had faith, or that there should be a word for me to act upon in faith. Therefore I was still sticking in the jaws of desperation, and went mourning up and down in a sad condition.

There was nothing now that I longed for more than to be put out of doubt as to this thing in question. As I was vehemently desiring to know if there was indeed hope for me, these words came rolling into my mind: *"Will the Lord cast off forever? And will he be favorable no more? Has His mercy ceased forever? Has His promise failed forevermore? Has God forgotten to be gracious? Has He in anger shut up His tender mercies?"* (Psalm 77:7-9). All the while they ran in my mind, I thought I had still this as the answer: it is a question whether He has or not, yet it may be He has not. Yes, the debate seemed to me to carry in it a sure affirmation that indeed He had not, nor would He so cast off, but would be favorable; that His promise does not fail; and that He has not forgotten to be gracious, nor would in anger shut up His tender mercy. Something also there was upon my heart at the same time, which I cannot now call to mind, with which this text did sweeten my heart and make me conclude that His mercy might not be quite gone, nor gone forever.

At another time I remember I was again much assailed with the question of whether the blood of Christ was sufficient to save my soul. I continued in this doubt from the early morning till about seven or eight at night. At last, when I was as it were quite worn out with fear that it would not lay hold on me, these words did sound suddenly within my heart, *"He is able"* (Hebrews 7:25). But I thought this word *able* was spoken aloud to me—a great word. It seemed to be written in great letters and gave such a jostle to my fear and doubt—I mean for the time it tarried with me, which was about a day—as I had never had from that all my life, either before or after.

But one morning, as I was again at prayer, and trembling under the fear of this, that no word of God could help me, that piece of a sentence darted in upon me, *"My grace is sufficient."* At this I thought I felt some relief, as if there might be hope. Oh, how good a thing it is for God to send his Word.

About a two weeks before I was looking on this very Scripture, and then I thought it could not come near my soul with comfort. Therefore I threw down my book in a huff. Then I thought it was not large enough for me—no, not large enough—but now it was as if it had arms of grace so wide that it could not only enclose me, but many more besides.

By these words I was sustained, yet not without exceeding conflicts, for the space of seven or eight weeks, for my peace would be in and out sometimes twenty times a day—comfort now, then trouble presently; peace now, but before I could go a furlong, as full of fear and guilt as ever a heart could hold. This was not only now and then, but for the whole seven weeks. This passage about the sufficiency of grace, and that of Esau's parting with his birthright, would be like a pair of scales within my mind: sometimes one end would be uppermost, and sometimes the other, according to which would be my peace or trouble.

Therefore I did still pray to God that He would come in with this Scripture more

fully on my heart, that He would help me
to apply the whole sentence, for as yet I
could not. What He gave me, that I gath-
ered, but further I could not go. As yet it
only helped me to hope there might be
mercy for me: *"My grace is sufficient."*
Though it came no further, it answered my
former question, if there was hope. Yet, because *"for you"* was left out, I was not
contented, but prayed to God for that also.

Thus one day, I was in a meeting of
God's people, full of sadness and terror, for
my fears again were strong upon me. As I
was now thinking my soul was never the
better, but my case most sad and fearful,
these words did with great power suddenly
break in upon me: *"My grace is sufficient
for you, My grace is sufficient for you, My
grace is sufficient for you,"* three times
altogether. Oh, I thought that every word
was a mighty word unto me, as *My*, and
grace, and *sufficient*, and *for you*; they were
then, and sometimes are still, far bigger
than others are.

At that time my understanding was so
enlightened that I felt as if I had seen the
Lord Jesus look down from heaven upon
me, and direct these words to me. This
thought sent me home mourning, for it

broke my heart, filled me full of joy, and laid me low as the dust. It did not stay long with me in this glory and refreshing comfort, yet it continued with me for several weeks and did encourage me to hope. But as soon as that powerful operation of it was taken from my heart, the verse about Esau returned to me as before. So my soul did hang as in the scales again—sometimes up and sometimes down, now in peace and again in terror.

Thus I went on for many weeks, sometimes comforted and sometimes tormented. Especially sometimes my torment would be very sore, for all those Scriptures aforenamed in Hebrews would be set before me, as the only sentences that would keep me out of heaven. Then, again, I would begin to repent that I ever thought like that.

I would also reason with myself: "Why, how many Scriptures are there against me? There are but three or four. Cannot God miss them and save me for all of them?" Sometimes, again, I would think, "Oh, if it were not for these three or four words, how might I be comforted." I could hardly forbear at times to wish them out of the Book.

Then I thought I saw that Peter and Paul and John and all the holy writers did look with scorn upon me and hold me in derision, as if they had said unto me, "All our words are truth, one of as much force as the other. It is not we that have cut you off, but you have cast away yourself. There is none of our sentences that you must take hold upon but these, and such as these: '*It is impossible.*' '*There no longer remains a sacrifice for sin.*' '*For it would have been better for them not to have known the way of righ-teousness, than having known it, to turn from the holy commandment delivered to them.*' '*The Scripture cannot be broken*'" (Hebrews 6:4; 10:26; 2 Peter 2:21; John 10:35).

As the elders of the city of refuge, I saw that they were to be the judges both of my case and me, while I stood with the avenger of blood at my heels, trembling at their gates for deliverance. Also with a thousand fears and mistrusts, I feared that they would shut me out forever (Joshua 20:3-4). Thus was I confounded, not knowing what to do or how to be satisfied in this question of whether the Scriptures could agree in the salvation of my soul. I quaked at the apostles; I knew their words were true, and that they must stand forever.

I remember one day, I was in various frames of spirit, according to the nature of several Scriptures that came into my mind —if this one of grace, then was I quiet; but if that of Esau, then tormented. Thought I, "Lord, if both these Scriptures should meet in my heart at once, I wonder which of them would get the better of me." So I thought I had a longing mind that they might both come together upon me. Yes, I desired of God they might.

Well, about two or three days afterward, they did indeed. They bolted both upon me at one time, and did work and struggle strongly in me for a while. At last that about Esau's birthright began to weaken and withdraw and vanish, and this about the sufficiency of grace prevailed with peace and joy.

As I was musing about this thing, that Scripture came into my mind, *"Mercy triumphs over judgment"* (James 2:13). This was a wonder to me, yet truly I am apt to think it was of God. The word of the law and wrath must give place to the word of life and grace, because, though the word of condemnation be glorious, yet the word of life and salvation far exceeds in glory (2 Corinthians 3:8-11).

This Scripture did also most sweetly visit my soul, *"And the one that comes to me I will by no means cast out"* (John 6:37). Oh, the comfort that I found from this word, *"by no means."* As if he had said, "By no means, for nothing, whatever he has done." But Satan would greatly labor to pull this promise from me by telling me that Christ did not mean me and such as I, but sinners of a lesser degree that had not done as I had done. But I would answer him again: "Satan, here in these words is no such exception; but *'one that comes'* —one, anyone—*'one that comes to me I will by no means cast out.'* "

This I well remember still, that of all the slights Satan used to take this Scripture from me, yet he never did so much as question me as to whether I came rightly. I have thought the reason was that because he thought I knew full well what coming rightly was. I saw that to come aright was to come as I was, a vile and ungodly sinner, and so cast myself at the feet of mercy, condemning myself for sin. If ever Satan and I did strive for any word of God in all my life, it was for this of Christ: he at one end, and I at the other. What a struggle we had! It was for this in John that we did so tug and strive: he pulled, and I pulled. But, God be praised, I overcame him. I got sweetness from it.

Notwithstanding all these helps and blessed words of grace, yet that of Esau's selling his birthright would still at times distress my conscience. Though I had been most sweetly comforted just before, yet when that Scripture came into my mind, it would make me fear again. I could not be rid of it, for it would return to haunt me.

Thus now I reasoned another way, even to consider the nature of my blasphemous thought. I meant to take the words at their largest and give them their own natural force and scope, every word of the thoght. So when I had thus considered, I found that if they were fairly taken, they would amount to this: I had freely left the Lord Jesus Christ to His choice, whether He would be my Savior or not, for the wicked words were these, "Let Him go if He will."

Then that Scripture gave me hope, *"I will never leave you, nor forsake you"* (Hebrews 13:5). "O Lord," said I, "but I have left You." Then it answered again, *"But I will never leave you."* For this I thanked God also. Yet I was grievously afraid He would, and found it exceeding hard to trust

Him, seeing I had so offended Him. I should have been exceeding glad that this thought had ever entered my mind, for then I thought I could have leaned on His grace with more ease and freedom in abundance. I saw it was with me as it was with Joseph's brothers: the guilt of their own wickedness did often fill them with fears that their brother would at last despise them (Genesis 50:15-16).

Yet above all the Scriptures that I yet did meet with, that in Joshua, chapter 20, was the greatest comfort to me, which speaks of the slayer that was to flee for refuge. If the avenger of blood pursue the slayer, then they that are the elders of the city of refuge *"shall not deliver the slayer into his hand, because he struck his neighbor unintentionally, but did not hate him beforehand"* (Joshua 20:5). Oh, blessed be God for this verse. I was convinced that I was the slayer, and that the avenger of blood pursued me I felt with great terror. It only now remained that I inquire whether I have the right to enter the city of refuge. So I found that he must not, *"who laid in wait to shed blood."* It was not the willful murderer, but he who unwittingly did it: he who did it unknowingly, not out of spite, or grudge, or malice, but he that shed it accidentally; even he who did not hate his neighbor before. Wherefore I thought, truly I was the man that must enter, because I had struck my neighbor *"unintentionally, but did not hate him beforehand."* I hated Him not before that time. No, I prayed unto Him, was tender about sinning against Him, and against this wicked temptation I fought for twelve months before. Also when it did pass through my heart, it did it in spite of my teeth. Wherefore I thought I had a right to enter this city, and the elders, which are the apostles, were not to deliver me up. This therefore was great comfort to me, and gave me much ground of hope.

Yet being very critical, for my logic had made me so that I knew not what ground was sure enough to bear me, I had one question that my soul did much desire to be resolved about: that was whether it was possible for any soul that had sinned the unpardonable sin to be able after that to receive even the least true spiritual comfort from God through Christ. After I had much considered the problem, I found the answer was that they could not, for these reasons:

First, those that have committed that sin cannot share in the blood of Christ. Being shut out of that, they must be devoid of the least ground of hope and so of spiritual comfort, for to such *there no longer remains a sacrifice for sins*" (Hebrews 10:26).

Secondly, because they have been denied a share in the promise of life, they *will not be forgiven, either in this age, or in the age to come*" (Matthew 12:32).

Thirdly, the Son of God excludes them also from sharing in His blessed intercession, being forever ashamed to own them, both before His holy Father and the blessed angels in heaven (Mark 8:38).

When I had with much deliberation considered this matter, and could not but conclude that the Lord had comforted me after this my wicked sin, then I thought I dared venture to come near those most fearful and terrible Scriptures with which all this while I had been so greatly frightened, and on which, before I had scarcely cast my eyes, I had struggled a hundred times to forbear wishing them out of the Bible because I feared they would destroy me. But now I say, I began to take some measure of encouragement to come close to them, to read them and consider them, and to weigh their scope and tendency. When I began to do so, I found their visage changed, for they looked not so grim as before I thought they did. First I came to the sixth chapter of Hebrews, yet trembling for fear it should strike me. When I had considered it, I found that the falling there intended was a falling quite away—that is, a falling from and an absolute denying of the Gospel of the remission of sins by Jesus Christ—for from them the apostle begins his argument. Also I found that this falling away must be open, even in the view of the world, so as *to put Christ to an open shame.* Further, I found that those there intended were forever shut up of God in blindness, hardness, and impenitency. *It is impossible they should be renewed again unto repentance.* By all these particulars I found, to God's everlasting praise, my sin was not the sin there intended.

First, I confessed I was fallen, but not fallen away from the profession of faith in Jesus unto eternal life.

Secondly, I confessed that I had put Jesus Christ to shame by my sin, but not to open shame; I did not deny Him before men, nor condemn Him as a fruitless one before the world.

Thirdly, I also did not find that God had shut me up or denied me to come— although I found it hard work indeed to come—to Him by sorrow and repentance. Blessed be God for unsearchable grace.

Then I considered the words in the tenth chapter of Hebrews, and found that the willful sin there mentioned is not every willful sin, but that which throws off Christ and His commandments, too. Secondly, that it must also be done openly, before two or three witnesses, to fulfill the demands of the law (Hebrews 10:28). Thirdly, this sin cannot be committed but with great spite done to the Spirit of grace —despising both the dissuasion from that sin and the persuasions to the contrary. The Lord knows, though this my sin was devilish, yet it did not amount to these.

As touching that in the twelfth chapter of Hebrews, about Esau's selling his birthright, though this was that which killed me and stood like a spear against me, yet now I did consider that his was not a hasty thought against the continual labor of his mind, but a thought consented to, and put in practice likewise, and that after some deliberation (Genesis 25:34). Further, it was a public and open action, even before his brother, if not before many more. This made his sin of a far more heinous nature than otherwise it would have been. Thirdly, he continued to slight his birthright: he did eat and drink and went his way. Thus Esau despised his birthright: yes, twenty years after, he was found to despise it still. *"And Esau said, I have enough, my brother; keep what you have for yourself"* (Genesis 33:9).

Now as touching this, that Esau sought a place of repentance, thus I thought:

First, this was not for the birthright, but the blessing. This is clear from the apostle and is distinguished by Esau himself, *"He took away my birthright, and now look, he has taken away my blessing!"* (Genesis 27:36).

Second, having thus considered, I came again to the apostle to see what might be the mind of God, in a New Testament style and sense, concerning Esau's sin. As far as I could conceive, this was the mind of God: that the birthright signified regeneration, and the blessing the eternal inheritance. So the apostle seems to hint: *"lest there be any fornicator or profane person like Esau, who for one morsel of food sold his birthright."* This is as if he was referring to whoever casts off all those blessed beginnings of God that at present are upon him as a consequence of the new birth, lest he becomes as Esau and even is rejected afterwards when he should inherit the blessing. For many there are who in the day of grace and mercy despise those things which are indeed the birthright to heaven, who, when the deciding day appears, will cry as loud as Esau, *"Lord, Lord, open for us"* (Luke 13:25). But just as Isaac would not relent, no more will God the Father, but will say, *"I have blessed him—and indeed he shall be blessed"* (Genesis 27:33), *"but as for you, depart from me, all you workers of iniquity."* (Luke 13:27).

When I had thus considered these Scriptures and found that to understand them thus was not against, but according to, other Scriptures, my encouragement and comfort were greatly increased. It also gave a great blow to that objection that the Scriptures could not agree in the salvation of my soul. And now remained only the afterpart of the tempest, for the thunder was gone beyond me, only some drops did still remain that now and then would fall upon me. But because my former frights and anguish were very sore and deep, it often befell me still as it befalls those that have been scared with fire. I thought every voice was, "Fire, fire." Every little touch would hurt my tender conscience.

But one day as I was passing into the field, with some dashes on my conscience, fearing yet that all was not right, suddenly this sentence fell upon my soul, "Your righteousness is in heaven." I thought I saw with the eyes of my soul Jesus Christ at God's right hand. There was my righteousness. Wherever I was, or whatever I was doing, God could not say of me that I lacked His righteousness, for that was ever before Him. Moreover, I saw that it was not my good frame of heart that made my righteousness better, nor yet my bad frame that made my righteousness worse, for my righteousness was Jesus Christ Himself, *the same yesterday, today, and forever* (Hebrews 13:8).

Now did my chains fall off my legs indeed. I was loosed from my afflictions and irons; my temptations also fled away. From that time those dreadful Scriptures of God quit troubling me; now went I also home rejoicing for the grace and love of God. So when I came home, I looked to see if I could find that sentence, "Your righteousness is in heaven," but could find no such saying. Wherefore my heart began to sink again, except that this was brought to my remembrance, *"But of Him you are in Christ Jesus, who became for us wisdom from God—and righteousness and sanctification and redemption"* (1 Corinthians 1:30). By this word I saw the other sentence was true; for by this Scripture I saw that the man Christ Jesus, as He is distinct from us as touching His bodily presence, so He is our righteousness and sanctification before God.

Here therefore I lived for some time very sweetly at peace with God, through Christ. I thought, "Oh, Christ, Christ!" There was nothing but Christ that was before my eyes. Now I was not only for looking upon one or another benefit of Christ separately, as of His blood, burial, or resurrection, but for considering Him as a whole Christ, as He in whom all these and all other His virtues, relations, offices, and operations met together, and that He sat on the right hand of God in heaven. It was glorious to me to see His exaltation and the worth and prevalence of all His benefits. Because now I could look from myself to Him, I would reckon that all those graces of God that now were newly on me were yet but like those cracked groats and fourpence-half-pennies that rich men carry in their purses when their gold is in their trunks at home. Oh, I saw my gold was in my trunk at home, in Christ my Lord and Savior. Now Christ was all— all my righteousness, all my sanctification, and all my redemption.

Further, the Lord did also lead me into the mystery of union with the soul of God —that I was joined to Him, that I was flesh of His flesh, and bone of his bone. Now was Ephesians 5:30 such a sweet word to me. By this also was my faith in Him as my righteousness the more confirmed in me: for if He and I were one, then His righteousness was mine, His merits mine, His victory also mine. Now I could see myself in heaven and earth at once—in heaven by my Christ, by my head, by my righteousness and life, though on earth in my body or person. Now I saw Christ Jesus was looked upon by God and should also be looked upon by us as that common or public Person in whom the whole body of His elect are always to be considered and reckoned—that we fulfilled the law by Him, died by Him, rose from the dead by Him, got the victory over sin, death, the devil, and hell by Him. When He died, we died; and so it is written of His resurrection, *"Your dead shall live; together with my dead body they shall rise"* (Isaiah 26:19). And again, *"After two days he will revive us; on the third day He shall raise us up that we may live in His sight"* (Hosea 6:2). This is now fulfilled by the sitting down of the Son of Man on the right hand of the Majesty in the heavens, according to that word to the Ephesians, *"He has raised us up together, and made us sit together in the heavenly places in Christ Jesus"* (Ephesians 2:6). Ah, these blessed considerations and Scriptures, with many others of like nature, were in those days made to sparkle in my eye, so that I have cause to say: *"Praise the Lord! Praise God in His sanctuary; praise Him in His mighty firmament! Praise Him for His mighty acts; praise Him according to His excellent greatness"* (Psalm 150:1-2).

Chapter Nine

Having thus, in few words, given you a taste of the sorrow and affliction that my soul endured by the guilt and terror that my wicked thoughts did subject me to, I have given you also a touch of my deliverance, and of the sweet and blessed comfort that I met with afterwards, which dwelt about twelve months with my heart to my unspeakable admiration. I will now, God willing, before I proceed any farther, give you in a word or two what I conceive was the cause of this temptation, and also after that, what advantage at the last it became unto my soul.

For the causes, I believe they were principally two, of which also I was deeply convinced all the time this trouble rested on me. The first was that I did not, when I was delivered from the first temptation, still pray to God to keep me from the temptations that were to come. For though, as I can say in truth, my soul was much in prayer before this trial seized me, yet I prayed only, or at the most principally, for the removal of present troubles and for fresh discoveries of His love in Christ, which I saw afterwards was not enough to do. I also should have prayed that the great God would keep me from the evil that was to come. Of this I was made deeply sensible by the prayer of holy David, who, when he was under present mercy, yet prayed that God would hold him back from sin and temptation to come: *"for then,"* says he, *"I shall be blameless, and I shall be innocent of great transgression"* (Psalm 19:13). By this very word was I vexed and condemned quite through this long temptation.

There was also another word that did much condemn me for my folly in the neglect of this duty: *"Let us therefore come boldly to the throne of grace, that we may obtain mercy and find grace to help in time of need"* (Hebrews 4:16). This I had not done, and was thus allowed to sin and fall, according to what is written: *"Rise and pray lest you enter into temptation"* (Luke 22:46). Truly this very thing is to this day of such weight and awe upon me that I dare not, when I come before the Lord, get up off my knees until I entreat Him for help and mercy against the temptations that are to come. And I do beseech you, reader, that you learn to beware of negligence from my afflictions that for this thing I did for days and months and years with sorrow undergo.

Another cause of this temptation was that I had tempted God. By this manner did I do it: at a time when my wife was great with child but before her full time was come, her pangs, as of a woman in travail, were fierce and strong upon her, even as she would have immediately fallen into labor and been delivered of an untimely birth. Now at this very time it was that I had been so strongly tempted to question the being of God. Wherefore, as my wife lay crying by me, I said with all secrecy imaginable, just thinking in my heart, "Lord, if now You will remove this sad affliction from my wife and cause her to be troubled no more this night"—at that moment were her pangs just upon her—"then shall I know that You can discern the most secret thoughts of the heart." I had no sooner said it in my heart but her pangs were taken from her, and she was cast into a deep sleep and so continued till morning. At this I greatly marveled, not knowing what to think. But after I had stayed awake a good while and heard her cry no more, I fell asleep also. So when I awoke the next morning it came upon me again what I had said in my heart the last night, and how the Lord had showed me that He knew my secret thoughts, which was a great astonishment to me for several weeks after.

Well, about a year and a half afterwards, that wicked, sinful thought of which I have spoken before went through my wicked heart, "Let Christ go if He will." So when I was fallen under guilt for this, the remembrance of my other thought, and of the effect thereof, would also come upon me with this retort, which also carried rebuke along with it: "Now you may see that God knows the most secret thoughts of the heart." And with this, the passages that were between the Lord and His servant Gideon fell upon my spirit: how because Gideon tempted God with his fleece, both wet and dry, when he should have believed and ventured upon His words, therefore the Lord did afterward so try him as to send him against an innumerable company of enemies, and that too, without any strength or help, as to outward appearance. (Judges 7:7). Thus He served me, and that justly. I should have believed His Word, and not have put an "if" upon the all-seeingness of God.

And now I desire to show you something of the advantages that I also gained by this temptation. First, by this I was made continually to possess in my soul a very wonderful sense both of the blessing and glory of God and of His beloved Son. In the temptation that went before, my soul was perplexed with unbelief, blasphemy, hardness of heart, and questions about the being of God, Christ, the truth of the Word, and certainly of the world to come. I say, then I was greatly assaulted and tormented with atheism, but now the case was otherwise. Now were God and Christ continually before my face, though not in a way of comfort, but in a way of exceeding dread and terror. The glory of the holiness of God did at this time break me to pieces, and the heart and compassion of Christ did break me as on the wheel, for I could not consider Him but as a lost and rejected Christ, the remembrance of which was as a continual breaking of my bones.

The Scriptures also were wonderful unto me. I saw that the truth and actuality of them were the keys of the kingdom of heaven: those that the Scriptures favor must inherit bliss, but those that they oppose and condemn must perish for evermore. Oh, this word, *"for the Scriptures cannot be broken,"* would rend the core of my heart, and so would that other: *"If you forgive the sins of any, they are forgiven them; if you retain the sins of any, they are retained"* (John 20:23). Now I saw the apostles to be the elders of the city of refuge (Joshua 20:4). Those that they were to receive in, were received to life; but those that they shut out, were to be slain by the avenger of blood. Oh, one sentence of the Scripture did more afflict and terrify my mind—I mean those sentences that stood against me, and sometimes I thought that every one did—more, I say, than an army of forty thousand men that might come against me. Woe be to him against whom the Scriptures bend themselves.

By this temptation I was made to see more into the nature of the promises than ever I had before, for I now lay trembling under the mighty hand of God, continually torn and rent by the thundering of His justice. This made me, with careful heart and watchful eye, with great fearfulness to turn over every leaf, and with much diligence mixed with trembling, consider every sentence, together with its natural force and latitude. By this temptation also I was greatly restrained from my former foolish practice of dismissing the word of promise when it came into my mind; for now, though I could not draw that comfort and sweetness from the promise which I had done at other times, yet, like a man sinking, I would catch at all I saw. Formerly I thought I might not muddle with the promise unless I felt its comfort, but now it was no time thus to do, so eagerly did the avenger of blood pursue me.

Now therefore was I glad to catch at that word, which yet I feared I had no ground or right to own, and even to leap into the bosom of that promise which yet I feared did shut its heart against me. Now also I would labor to take the Word as God had set it down, without restraining the natural force of one syllable thereof. Oh, what did I see in the blessed sixth chapter of John, *"And the one who comes to Me I will by no means cast out"* (John 6:37). Now I began to consider with myself that God had a bigger mouth to speak with than I had a heart to conceive with. I thought also with myself that He spoke not His words in haste or in an unadvised heat, but with infinite wisdom and judgment, and in all truth and faithfulness.

I would in these days often, in my greatest agonies, even lurch towards the promise—as the horses do towards sound ground and yet stick in the mire—concluding, though as one almost bereft of his wits through fear, on this will I rest and stay and leave the fulfilling of it to the God of heaven that said it. Oh, many a fight had my heart had with Satan for that blessed sixth chapter of John. I did not now, as at other times, look principally for comfort, though how welcome would it have been unto me. But now a word, a word to lean a weary soul upon, that it might not sink forever, was what I hunted. Yes, often when I have been looking to the promise, it seemed as if the Lord would refuse my soul forever. It was as if I had run upon the pikes, and as if the Lord had thrust at me to keep me from Him as with a flaming sword. Then would I think of Esther, who went to petition the king contrary to the law. I thought also of Ben-Hadad's servants, who went with ropes upon their heads to their enemies for mercy. The woman of Canaan also, that would not be daunted though called a dog by Christ, and the man that went to borrow bread at midnight were also great encouragements unto me. (See Esther 4:16; 1 Kings 20:31ff; Matthew 15:22ff; Luke 11:5-8.)

I never saw such heights and depths in grace and love and mercy as I saw after this temptation—great sins to draw out great grace. Where guilt is most terrible and fierce, there the mercy of God in Christ, when shown to the soul, appears most high and mighty. When Job had passed through his captivity, he had twice as much as he had before (Job 42:10). Blessed be God for Jesus Christ our Lord. Many other things I might here make observation of, but I would be brief, and therefore shall at this time omit them. I pray to God that my sins may make others fear to offend, lest they also be made to bear the iron yoke as I did. I had two or three times, at or about my deliverance from this temptation, such strange apprehensions of the grace of God, that I could hardly bear up under it. It was so out of measure amazing, when I thought it could reach me, that I do think if that sense of it had stayed long upon me it would have made me incapable for business.

Now I shall go forward to relate to you some other of the Lord's dealings with me at other seasons and of the temptations I then did meet overall. I shall begin with what I met with when first I joined in fellowship with the people of God in Bedford. I had propounded to the church that my desire was to walk in the order and ordinances of Christ with them, and had been also admitted by them.

During this time when I thought of the blessed ordinance of Christ which was His last supper with His disciples before His death, the Scripture, *"Do this in remembrance of Me"* (Luke 22:19), was made very precious to me. By it the Lord came upon my conscience with the discovery of His death for my sins, and as I then felt, it was as if He plunged me in the virtue of the same. But behold, I had not been long a partaker in that ordinance, when such a fierce and sad temptation did attend me at all times during it, both to blaspheme the ordinance and to wish some deadly thing to those that then did partake. Lest I should at any time be guilty of consenting to these wicked and fearful thoughts, I was forced to bend myself all the while to pray to God to keep me from such blasphemies, and also to cry to God to bless the cup and bread to them, as it were, from mouth to mouth. The reason of this temptation, I have thought since, was because I did not approach to partake with that same reverence that became me at first. Thus I continued for three quarters of a year and could never have rest nor ease, but at the last the Lord came in upon my soul with that same Scripture by which my soul was visited before. After that I have been usually very well and comfortable in the partaking of that blessed ordinance, and have, I trust, discerned the Lord's body as broken for my sins and that His precious blood has been shed for my transgressions.

One spring for a time, I was somewhat inclined to consumption, with which I was suddenly and violently seized with much weakness in my outward man, insomuch that I thought I could not live. Now began I afresh to give myself up to a serious examination of my state and condition for the future and of my evidences for that blessed world to come. It has, I bless the name of God, been my usual course, especially in the day of affliction, to endeavor to keep my interests in the life to come clear before my eyes. But I had no sooner begun to recall to mind my former experience of the goodness of God to my soul, than there came flocking into my mind an innumerable company of my sins and transgressions. Among these at this time, most to my sorrow, were, namely, my deadness, dullness, and coldness in my holy duties; my wanderings of heart, my wearisomeness in all good things; my lack of love to God, His ways, and people. At the end of all was: "Are these the fruits of Christianity? Are these the tokens of a blessed man?"

At the apprehensions of these things my sickness was doubled upon me, for now I was sick also in my inward man, my soul being clogged with guilt. Now also were my former experiences of God's goodness to me quite taken out of my mind and hidden, as if they had never been or seen. Now was my soul greatly pinched between these two considerations: "Live I must not; die I dare not." Now I sunk and fell in my spirit, and was giving up all for lost. But as I was walking up and down my house as a man in a most woeful state, that word of God took hold of my heart: *You being justified freely by His grace through the redemption that is in Christ Jesus*" (Romans 3:24). But what a turn it made upon me. Now was I

148

as one awakened out of some troublesome sleep and dream. And listening to this heavenly sentence, it was as if I had heard spoken to me: "Sinner, you think that because of your sins and infirmities I cannot save your soul; but behold, my Son is by Me, and upon Him I look, and not on you, and shall deal with you according to My pleasure with Him." At this I was greatly enlightened in my mind and made to understand that God could justify a sinner at any time; it was but His looking upon Christ and imputing His benefits to us, and the work was forthwith done.

As I was thus in a muse, that Scripture also came with great power upon my spirit: *"Who has saved us and called us with a holy calling, not according to our works, but according to His purpose and grace"* (2 Timothy 1:9). Now was I seated on high; I saw myself within the arms of grace and mercy. Though I was before afraid to think of a dying hour, yet now I cried, "Let me die." Now death was lovely and beautiful in my sight, for I saw we shall never live indeed till we are gone to the other world. Oh, this life is but a slumber in comparison with that above. At this time also I saw more in these words, *"heirs of God"*

(Romans 8:17), than ever I shall be able to express while I live in this world. Heirs of God! God himself is the portion of the saints. This I saw and wondered at, but cannot tell you what I saw.

Again, I was at another time very ill and weak, all that time also the tempter besetting me strongly—for I find he is much for assaulting the soul when it begins to approach towards the grave, for then is his opportunity—laboring to hide from me my former experience of God's goodness. He was also setting before me the terrors of death and the judgment of God, insomuch that at this time, through my fear of miscarrying forever should I now die, I was as one dead before death came, and was as if I had felt myself already descending into the pit. I thought I said, "There is no way, but to hell I go." But behold, just as I was in the middle of those fears, these words of the angels carrying Lazarus into Abraham's bosom darted in upon me, as if to say, "So shall it be with you when you shall leave this world." This sweetly revived my spirits and helped me to hope in God. When I had with comfort mused on this awhile, that word fell with great weight upon my mind: *"O death, where is your sting? O Hades, where is your victory?"* (1 Corinthians 15:55). At this I became both well in body and mind at once, for my sickness did presently vanish, and I walked comfortably in my work for God again.

At another time, although just before I was pretty well and strong in my spirit, yet suddenly there fell upon me a great cloud of darkness, which did so hide from me the things of God and Christ that it was as if I had never seen or known them in my life. I was also so overrun in my soul with a senseless, heartless frame of spirit, that I could not feel my soul move or stir after grace and life by Christ. It was as if my loins were broken, or as if my hands and feet had been tied and bound with chains. At this time also I felt some weakness seize upon my outward man, which made still the other affliction all the more heavy and uncomfortable to me.

After I had been in this condition some three or four days, as I was sitting by the fire, I suddenly felt this word sound in my heart, "I must go to Jesus." At this my former darkness and atheism fled away, and the blessed things of heaven were set in my view. While I was on this, suddenly thus overtaken with surprise, "Wife," said

I, "is there ever such a Scripture, 'I must go to Jesus'?" She said she was not sure; therefore I stood musing still, to see if I could remember such a verse. I had not sat more than two or three minutes but there came bolting in upon me, *"To an innumerable company of angels"* (Hebrews 12:22), and the whole twelfth chapter of Hebrews, about the mount Zion, was set before my eyes. Then with joy I told my wife, "Oh, now I know, I know." That night was a good night for me; I have had but few better. I longed for the company of some of God's people, that I might impart unto them what God had showed me. Christ was a precious Christ to my soul that night. I could scarcely lie in my bed for joy and peace and triumph through Christ.

This great glory did not continue upon me until morning, yet the twelfth chapter of the epistle to the Hebrews was a blessed Scripture to me for many days after this. The words are these: *"But you have come to Mount Zion, and to the city of the living God, the heavenly Jerusalem, to an innumerable company of angels, to the general assembly and church of the first-born, who are registered in heaven, and to God, the Judge of all, to the spirits of just men made perfect, to Jesus the Mediator of the new covenant, and to the blood of sprinkling, that speaks better things than that of Abel"* (Hebrews 12:22-24). Through this sentence the Lord led me over and over, first to this word and then to that, and showed me wonderful glory in every one of them. These words also have often since that time been great refreshment to my spirit. Blessed be God for having mercy on me.

Chapter Ten

Now since I am speaking about my experience, I will here thrust in a word or two concerning my preaching the Word, and of God's dealing with me in that particular also. After I had been awakened about five or six years, and had been helped myself to see both the need and worth of Jesus Christ our Lord, and also enabled to venture my soul upon Him, some of the most able among the saints with us—I say, the most able for judgment and holiness of life as they conceived—did perceive that God had counted me worthy to understand something of His will in His holy and blessed Word, and had given me utterance in some measure to express what I saw to others for edification. Therefore they desired, and that with much earnestness, that I would be willing sometimes to speak in one of the meetings a word of exhortation unto them. Though at the first it did much dash and abash my spirit, yet being still by them desired and entreated,

I consented to their requests and did so twice, at two different assemblies, but in private, though with much weakness and infirmity, discover my gifts among them. They not only seemed to be, but did frequently insist, in the sight of the great God, that they were both affected and comforted by this my gifting. And they gave thanks to the Father of mercies for the grace bestowed on me. After this, sometimes when some of them went into the country to teach, they wanted also that I would go with them. Though as yet I did not and dared not make use of my gifts in an open way, yet more privately still, as I came among the good people in those places, I did sometimes speak a word of admonition unto them also. They, as the others, received the word with rejoicing at the mercy of God toward me, professing their souls were edified thereby.

Wherefore, at last being still desired by the church, after some solemn prayer to the Lord with fasting, I was more particularly called forth and appointed to a more ordinary and public preaching of the Word, not only to and among them that believed, but also to offer the Gospel to those who had not yet received the faith. About that time I did evidently find in my mind a secret inclination thereto, though, I bless God, not for a desire of vainglory, for at that time I was most sorely afflicted with the fiery darts of the devil concerning my eternal state.

But yet I could not be content unless I was found in the exercise of my gift, unto which also I was greatly animated, not only by the continual desires of the godly, but also by that saying of Paul to the Corinthians: *"I urge you, brethren—you know the household of Stephanas, that it is the first-fruits of Achaia, and that they have devoted themselves to the ministry of the saints—that you also submit to such, and to everyone who works and labors with us"* (1 Corinthians 16:15-16). By this text I was made to see that the Holy Ghost never intended that men who have gifts and abilities should bury them in the earth, but rather did command and stir up such to the exercise of their gift, and also did commend those that are apt and ready so to do. *"They have devoted themselves to the ministry of the saints."* This Scripture in these days did continually run in my mind to encourage me and strengthen me in my work for God. I have also been encouraged from several other Scriptures and examples of the godly, both specified in the Word and in other ancient histories. (See Acts 8:4; 18:24-25; 1 Peter 4:10; Romans 12:6; and Foxe's *Book of Martyrs*).

Wherefore, though of myself of all the saints the most unworthy, yet I, with great fear and trembling at the sight of my weakness, did set upon the work and did, according to my gifts and the proportion of my faith, preach that blessed Gospel that God had showed me in the Holy Word of Truth. When the country understood, they came in to hear the Word by hundreds, and that from all parts, though for various and sundry reasons. And I thank God He gave unto me some measure of compassion and pity for their souls, which also did put me forward to labor with great diligence and earnestness to find such a word as might, if God would bless it, lay hold of and awaken the conscience. In which efforts the good Lord respected the desire of His servant, for I had not preached long before some began to be touched and be greatly afflicted in their minds at the apprehension of the greatness of their sin and of their need of Jesus Christ.

I first could not believe that God should speak by me to the heart of any man, still counting myself unworthy. Yet those who were thus touched would love me and have a particular respect for me. Though I did put it from me that they should be awakened by me, still they would confess and affirm it before the saints of God. They would also bless God for this unworthy wretch, and count me God's instrument that showed to them the way of salvation.

Wherefore, seeing them in both their words and deeds to be so constant, and also in their hearts so earnestly pressing after the knowledge of Jesus Christ, rejoicing that God did send me where they were, then I began to conclude it might be so, that God had owned in His work such a foolish one as I. Then came that word of God to my heart with much sweet refreshment: *"The blessing of a perishing man came upon me, and I caused the widow's heart to sing for joy"* (Job 29:13). At this therefore I rejoiced; yes, the tears of those whom God did awaken by my preaching would be both solace and encouragement to me. I thought on these Scriptures: *"Who is he who makes me glad but the one who is made sorrowful by me?"* (2 Corinthians

2:2), and again, *"If I am not an apostle to others, yet doubtless I am to you. For you are the seal of my apostleship in the Lord"* (1 Corinthians 9:2). These things therefore were as another argument unto me that God had called me and stood by me in this work.

In my preaching of the Word, I took special notice of this one thing, namely, that the Lord did lead me to begin where his Word begins—with sinners—to condemn all flesh, and to open and allege that the curse of God by the law does belong to and lay hold of all men as they come into the world, because of sin. Now this part of my work I fulfilled with great earnestness, for the terrors of the law and guilt for my transgressions lay heavy on my conscience. I preached what I felt, what I smartingly did feel, even that under which my poor soul did groan and tremble in astonishment. Indeed, I have been as one sent to them from the dead. I went, myself in chains, to preach to them in chains, and carried that fire in my own conscience that I persuaded them to be aware of. I can truly say, without disguising, that when I have gone to preach, I have gone full of guilt and terror, even to the pulpit door.

There it has been taken off, and I have been at liberty in my mind until I have done my work. Then immediately, even before I could get down the pulpit stairs, I have been as bad as I was before. Yet God carried me on, but surely with a strong hand, for neither guilt nor hell could take me from my work.

Thus I went on for the space of two years, crying out against men's sins, and their fearful state because of them. After that the Lord came in upon my soul with some sure peace and comfort through Christ, for He did give me many sweet discoveries of His blessed grace through Him. Then I altered in my preaching, for still I preached what I saw and felt. Now therefore I did much labor to hold forth Jesus Christ in all His offices, relations, and benefits unto the world, and did strive also to discover, to condemn, and to remove those false supports and props on which the world does lean, and by which they fall and perish. On these things also I stayed as long as on the other.

After this God led me into something of the mystery of the union of Christ, which I discovered and showed to them also. And when I had traveled through these three

chief points of the Word of God, in about
the space of five years or so, I was caught
in my present practice and cast into prison,
where I have remained for as long again, to
confirm the truth by way of suffering, as I
was before in testifying of it according to
the Scriptures by way of preaching. When
I have been preaching, I thank God my
heart has often, with great earnestness, of
this and the other exercises, cried to God
that He would make the word effectual to
the salvation of souls, still being grieved
lest the enemy should take the word away
from the conscience, and thus it should
become unfruitful. Wherefore I labored so
to speak the word as that thereby, if it
were possible, the sin and person guilty
might be particularized by it.

Also, when I have done the exercise, it
has gone to my heart to think the word
should now fall as rain on stony places,
still wishing from my heart, "Oh, that they
who have heard me speak this day did but
see as I do what sin, death, hell, and the
curse of God are; and also what the grace
and love and mercy of God are, through
Christ, to men in such a case as they are,
who are yet estranged from Him." And
indeed I did often say in my heart before

the Lord, that if to be hanged up presently before their eyes would be a means to awaken them and confirm them in the truth, I gladly should consent to it; for it has been in my preaching, especially when I have been engaged in the doctrine of life by Christ without works, as if an angel of God had stood by at my back to encourage me. Oh, it has been with such power and heavenly evidence upon my own soul while I have been laboring to unfold it, to demonstrate it, and to fasten it upon the consciences of others, that I could not be contented with just saying that I believe and am sure. I thought I was more than sure, if it be lawful so to express myself, that those things which then I asserted were true.

When I first went to preach the Word abroad, the doctors and priests of the country did open wide against me. But I was persuaded of this, not to render railing for railing, but to see how many of these carnal professors I could convince of their miserable state by the law, and of the need and worth of Christ. I thought that this shall answer for me in time to come, when they shall be for my hire before their face (Genesis 30:33). I never cared to meddle

with things that were controverted and in
dispute among the saints, especially things
of the lowest nature. Yet it pleased me
much to contend with great earnestness for
the word of faith, and remission of sins by
the death and sufferings of Jesus. But, I
say as to other things, I would let them
alone, because I saw they engendered
strife, and because they neither in doing
nor in leaving undone did commend us to
God to be His. Besides, I saw my work
before me was directed in another channel,
even to carry an awakening word. To that,
therefore, I did stick and adhere. I never
endeavored to nor dared make use of other
men's lines (Romans 15:18), though I condemn not all that do, for I truly thought
and found by experience that what was
taught me by the Word and Spirit of Christ
could be spoken, maintained, and stood to
by the soundest and best established conscience. Though I will not now speak all
that I know in this matter, yet my experience has more interest in that text of
Galatians 1:11-12, than many among men
are aware.

If any of those who were awakened by
my ministry did afterwards fall back, as
sometimes too many did, I can truly say

their loss has been more to me than if my own children, begotten of my own body, had been going to their grave. I think truly I may speak it without offense to the Lord, nothing has gone so near me as that, unless it was the fear of the loss of the salvation of my own soul. I have counted as if I had goodly buildings and lordships in those places where my children were born.

My heart has been so wrapped up in the glory of this excellent work, that I counted myself more blessed and honored of God than if he had made me the emperor of the Christian world or the lord of all the glory of the earth without it. *"He that turns a sinner from the error of his way will save a soul from death"* (James 5:20). *"The fruit of the righteous is a tree of life; and he who wins souls is wise"* (Proverbs 11:30). *"Those who are wise shall shine like the brightness of the firmament; and those who turn many to righteousness, like the stars forever and ever"* (Daniel 12:3). *"For what is our hope, or joy, or crown of rejoicing? Is it not even you in the presence of our Lord Jesus Christ at His coming? For you are our glory and joy"* (1 Thessalonians 2:19-20). These and others of a like nature, have been great refreshments to me.

I have observed that where I have had a work to do for God, I have had first, as it were, the going of God upon my spirit to desire I might preach there. I have also observed that certain souls in particular have been strongly set upon my heart, and I was stirred up to wish for their salvation, those very souls having after this been given as the fruits of my ministry. I have observed that a word interjected in passing has done more execution in a sermon than all that was spoken besides. Sometimes also, when I have thought I did no good, then I did most of all. At other times, when I thought I should catch them, I have fished for nothing.

I have also observed that where there has been a work to do upon sinners, there the devil has begun to roar in the hearts and by the mouths of his servants; yes, often times when the wicked world has raged most, there have been souls awakened by the Word. I could tell particular instances, but I forbear.

My great desire in my fulfilling my ministry was to get into the darkest places of the country, even among those people that were farthest away from salvation. Yet this was not because I could not endure the light, for I feared not to show my Gospel to any, but because I found my spirit did lean most after awakening and converting work, and the message that I carried did lean itself most that way also. *"And so I have made it my aim to preach the gospel, not where Christ was named, lest I should build upon another man's foundation"* (Romans 15:20).

In my preaching I have really been in pain, and have, as it were, travailed to bring forth children to God. Neither could I be satisfied unless some fruits did appear in my work. If I were fruitless, it mattered not who commended me; but if I were fruitful, I cared not who condemned. I have thought of that: *"Behold, children are a heritage of the Lord, the fruit of the womb is His reward. Like arrows in the hand of a mighty man, so are the children of one's youth. Happy is the man that has his quiver full of them; they shall not be ashamed, but they shall speak with their enemies in the gate"* (Psalm 127:3-5). It pleased me nothing to see people drink in my opinions, if they seemed ignorant of Jesus Christ and the worth of their own salvation. Sound conviction for sin, especially for unbelief, and a heart set on fire to be saved by

Christ, with strong yearning after a truly sanctified soul, this it was that delighted me. Those were the souls I counted blessed.

But in this work, as in all others, I had my temptations attending me, and that of various kinds. Sometimes I would be assaulted with great discouragement, fearing that I should not be able to speak a word at all to edification, or more, that I should not be able to speak sense to the people. At these times I would have such a strange faintness and lack of strength seize upon my body that my legs were scarcely able to carry me to the place of exercise.

Sometimes, again, when I have been preaching, or have been violently assaulted with thoughts of blasphemy, and strongly tempted to speak the words with my mouth before the congregation, I have also at times—even when I have begun to speak the word with much clearness, evidence, and liberty of speech—yet been, before the ending of that opportunity, so blinded and so estranged from the things I have been speaking, and have been also so strained in my speech as to utterance before the people, that it has been as if I had not known or remembered what I have been about, or as if my head had been in a bag all the time of my exercise.

Again, when sometimes I have been about to preach upon some smart and searching portion of the word, I have found the tempter suggest, "What, will you preach this? This condemns yourself; of this your own soul is guilty; wherefore preach not of this at all—or if you do—yet so mince it as to make way for your own escape, lest, instead of awakening others, you lay that guilt upon your own soul that you will never get out from under." But, thank the Lord, I have been kept from consenting to these horrid suggestions, and have rather, as Samson, bowed myself with all my might to condemn sin and transgression wherever I found it. Yes, even though I did bring guilt upon my own conscience, I thought, *Let me die with the Philistines* (Judges 16:30), rather than deal corruptly with the blessed Word of God. *You therefore who teach another, do you not teach yourself?* (Romans 2:21). It is far better then to judge yourself, even by preaching plainly unto others, than that to save yourself, imprison the truth in unrighteousness. Blessed be God for His help also in this.

I have also, while found in this blessed work of Christ, been often tempted to pride and lifting up of heart. Though I dare not say I have not been affected with this, yet truly the Lord in His precious mercy has so dealt with me, that for the most part, I have had but small desire to give way to such a thing, for it has been my every day's portion to be let into the evil of my own heart, and still made to see such a multitude of corruptions and infirmities therein, that it has caused hanging down of the head under all my gifts and attainments. I have felt this thorn in the flesh the very mercy of God to me (2 Corinthians 12:8).

Together with this thorn, I have also had some notable reference or other in the Word before me, which has contained in it some sharp and piercing sentence concerning the perishing of the soul, notwithstanding gifts and parts. For instance, these words have been of great use to me, *"Though I speak with the tongues of men and of angels, and have not love, I have become as sounding brass or a clanging cymbal"* (1 Corinthians 13:1-2). A tinkling cymbal is an instrument of music with which a skilful player can make such melodious and heart-inflaming music, that all who hear him play can scarcely refrain from dancing. Yet, behold, the cymbal does not have life, neither does the music come from it, except by the art of him that plays it. So then the instrument at last may come to nothing and perish, though in times past such music has been made upon it. Just thus I saw it was and will be with them that have gifts but lack saving grace: they are in the hand of Christ as the cymbal in the hand of David. As David could with the cymbal make such mirth in the service of God as to elevate the hearts of the worshipers, so Christ can so use these gifted men to affect the souls of His people in the church, and yet when He has done all, lay them by as lifeless though sounding cymbals.

This consideration therefore, together with some others, was for the most part as a maul on the head of pride and desire for vainglory. Thought I, "Shall I be proud because I am as sounding brass? Is it so much to be a fiddle? Has not the least creature that has life more of God in it than these?" Besides, I knew it was love that should never die, but these must cease and vanish. So I concluded a little grace, a little love, a little of the true fear of God, is better than all gifts. I am fully convinced that it is possible for souls, who can scarcely give a man an answer but with great confusion as to method, to have a thousand times more grace and so be more in the love and favor of the Lord, than some who by the virtue of the gift of knowledge can deliver themselves like angels.

Thus, therefore, I came to perceive that though gifts in themselves were good to the thing for which they are designed—the edification of others—yet they are empty and without power to save the soul of him that has them, if they be alone. Neither are they any sign of a man's state to be happy, being only a dispensation of God to some, of whose improvement or non-improvement they must, when a little more time is over, give an account to Him that is ready to judge the quick and the dead. This slowed me too, that gifts being alone were dangerous, not in themselves, but because of those evils that attend those that have them —pride, desire for vainglory, self-conceit, and so on—all which were easily blown up at the applause and commendation of every unadvised Christian, to the endangering of a poor creature to fall into the condemnation of the devil.

I saw, therefore, that he that has gifts had need to be let into a view of the nature of them—that they come short of making him to be in a truly saved condition—lest he rest in them and so fall short of the grace of God. He has cause also to walk humbly with God and be little in his own eyes, and to remember that his gifts are not his own, but the church's, and that by them he is made a servant to the church. He must give at last an account of his stewardship unto the Lord Jesus. To give a good account will be a blessed thing. Let all men therefore prize a little with the fear of the Lord: gifts indeed are desirable, but yet great grace and small gifts are better than great gifts and no grace. It does not say the Lord gives gifts and glory, but the Lord gives grace and glory. Blessed is such a one to whom the Lord gives grace, true grace, for that is a certain forerunner of glory.

But when Satan perceived that his thus tempting and assaulting me would not answer his design to overthrow the ministry and make it ineffectual as to the ends thereof, then he tried another way, which was to stir up the minds of the ignorant and malicious to load me with slanders and reproaches. Now I may say that whatever the devil could devise and his instruments invent was whirled up and down the country against me, thinking, as I said, that by that means they should make my ministry to be abandoned. It began therefore to be rumored up and down among the people that I was a witch, a Jesuit, a highwayman, and the like. To all of which, I shall only say, God knows that I am innocent. But as for my accusers, let them provide themselves to meet me before the tribunal of the Son of God, there to answer for all these things, with all the rest of their iniquities, unless God shall give them repentance for their sins, for which I pray with all my heart.

But that which was reported with the boldest confidence was that I was addicted to gross immoralities and the like. Now these slanders, with the others, I glory in, because they are but slanders, foolish or scheming lies and falsehoods cast upon me by the devil and his seed; and should I not be dealt with thus wickedly by the world, I should lack one of the signs of a saint and a child of God. *"Blessed are you,"* says the Lord, *"when they revile and persecute you, and say all kinds of evil against you falsely for My sake. Rejoice and be exceedingly glad, for great is your reward in heaven, for so they persecuted the prophets who were before you"* (Matthew 5:11-12).

These things therefore for my personal account trouble me not, even if they were twenty times more than they are. I have a good conscience. Whereas they speak evil of me as an evil-doer, they shall be ashamed that falsely accuse my good conversation in Christ. So then, what shall I say to those who have thus bespattered me? Shall I threaten them? Shall I chide them? Shall I flatter them? Shall I entreat them to hold their tongues? No, not I. Were it not that these things make those who are the authors and abettors ripe for damnation, I would say unto them, "Report it, because it will increase my glory." Therefore I bind these lies and slanders to me as an ornament: it belongs to my Christian profession to be vilified, slandered, reproached, and reviled. Since all this is nothing else, as my God and my conscience do bear me witness, I rejoice in reproaches for Christ's sake.

I also call upon all those fools and knaves that have thus made it any part of their business to affirm any of these things forenamed of me, namely, that I have been of unchaste life or the like, when they have used the utmost of their endeavors and made the fullest inquiry that they call, to prove against me truly that there is any one in heaven, or earth, or hell that can say I have at any time, in any place, by day or night, so much as attempted any unbecoming familiarity. Do I speak thus to beg mine enemies into a good esteem of me? No, not I. I will in this beg belief of no man: believe or disbelieve me in this, all is a similar case to me. My foes have missed their mark in their shooting at me. I am not the man. I wish that they themselves were guiltless. If all the fornicators and adulterers in England were hanged up by the neck till they be dead, John Bunyan, the object of their envy, would be still alive and well. I know not whether there is such a thing as a woman breathing under the canopy of the heaven except by their apparel, their children, or by common fame, except my wife.

And in this I admire the wisdom of God, that he made me in this respect circumspect from my first conversion until now. They, with whom I have been most intimately concerned, know and can also bear me witness that it is a rare thing to see me to behave familiarly toward any female. The common salutation I abhor—it is odious to me in whomsoever I see it. Their company alone I cannot approve, for I think these things are not becoming to me. When I have seen good men salute those women that they have visited, or that have visited them, I have at times made my objection against it. And when they have answered that it was but a piece of civility, I have told them it was not a comely sight. Some indeed have urged the *"holy kiss,"* but then I have asked why they have made such exceptions—why they did salute the most handsome, and let the ill-favored go. Thus, however laudable such things have been in the eyes of others, they have been unseemly in my sight.

And now for a ending in this matter. I call not only on men but angels to prove me guilty of having broken the marriage covenant; nor am I afraid to do it a second time, knowing that I cannot offend the Lord in such a case to call on God for a record upon my soul that in these things I am innocent. Not that I have been thus kept because of any goodness in me more than any other, but God has been merciful to me and has kept me. I pray that He will keep me still, not only from this, but every evil way and work, and preserve me to His heavenly kingdom. Amen.

Now, as Satan labored by reproaches and slanders to make me vile among my countrymen, that if possible my preaching might be made of none effect, so there was added thereto a long and tedious imprisonment, that thereby I might be frightened from my service for Christ and the world made afraid to hear me preach, of which I shall next give you a brief account.

Chapter Eleven

Having made my profession of the glorious Gospel of Christ for a long time and preached the same for about five years, I was apprehended at a meeting of good people in the country, among whom, had they let me alone, I would have preached that day. But they took me away from among them and had me before a justice, who, after I had offered security for my appearing at the next session of the courts, yet they committed me to prison because my sureties would not consent to be bound that I should preach no more to the people.

At the session afterward, I was indicted as an upholder and maintainer of unlawful assemblies and conventions, and for not conforming to the national worship of the church of England. After some conference there with the justices, they, taking my plain dealing with them for a confession, as they termed it, of the indictment, did sentence me to perpetual banishment because

I refused to conform. So being delivered up to the jailer's hand, I was taken to prison, and there have remained now complete for twelve years, waiting to see what God would allow those men to do with me. In this condition I have continued with much content, through grace, but have met with many turnings and goings upon my heart, both from the Lord, Satan, and my own corruption. By all which—glory be to Jesus Christ—I have also received among many things much conviction, instruction, and understanding, of which at length I shall not here discourse, but only give you a hint or two—a word that may stir up the godly to bless God and to pray for me, and also to take encouragement, should the case be their own, not to fear what man can do unto them.

I never had in all my life so great an insight into the Word of God as now. Those Scriptures that I saw nothing in before, were made in this place and state to shine upon me. Jesus Christ also was never more real and apparent than now: here I have seen and felt Him indeed. This verse, *"We did not follow cunningly devised fables when we made known to you the power and coming of our Lord Jesus Christ"* (2 Peter

1:16), and that, *"God who raised Him from the dead and gave Him glory, so that your faith and hope are in God"* (1 Peter 1:21), were blessed words unto me in this imprisoned condition. These three or four Scriptures also have been great refreshments in this condition to me: John 14:1-4; 16:33; Colossians 3:3-4; and Hebrews 12:22-24. Sometimes when I have enjoyed the savor of them, I have been able to laugh at destruction, and to fear neither the horse nor his rider.

I have had sweet sights of the forgiveness of my sins in this place, and of my being with Jesus in another world. Oh, the mount Zion, the heavenly Jerusalem, the innumerable company of angels, and God the Judge of all, and the spirits of just men made perfect, and Jesus, have been sweet unto me in this place. I have seen that here, which I am persuaded I shall never while in this world be able to express. I have seen a truth in this Scripture: *"Whom having not seen, you love. Though now you do not see Him, yet believing, you rejoice with joy inexpressible and full of glory"* (1 Peter 1:8). I never knew what it was for God to stand by me at all times and at every offer of Satan to afflict me, as I have found Him since I came in to this place, for as fears have presented themselves, so have supports and encouragements. Yes, when I have been startled, even as it were at nothing else but my shadow, yet God, being very tender to me, has not suffered me to be molested, but would with one Scripture or another strengthen me against all. To such an extent has this been true that I have often said that were it lawful, I would pray for greater trouble for the greater comfort's sake (Ecclesiastes 7:14; 2 Corinthians 1:5).

Before I came to prison, I saw what was coming and had especially two considerations warm upon my heart. The first was, how to be able to encounter death, should that be here my portion. For this that Scripture was great information to me, namely, to pray to God to be *strengthened with all might, according to His glorious power, for all patience and long-suffering with joy*" (Colossians 1:11). I could seldom go to prayer for a full year before I was imprisoned, but this sentence or sweet petition would, as it were, thrust itself into my mind, and persuade me that if ever I would go through long-suffering, I must have patience, especially if I would endure it joyfully.

As to the second consideration, this Scripture was of great use to me: *"Yes, we had the sentence of death in ourselves, that we should not trust in ourselves but in God who raises the dead"* (2 Corinthians 1:9). By this verse I was made to see that if ever I would suffer rightly, I must first pass a sentence of death upon everything that can be properly called a thing of this life, even to reckon myself, my wife, my children, my health, my enjoyment, and all, as dead to me, and myself as dead to them.

The second was, to live unto God that is invisible, as Paul said in another place. The way not to faint is, *"do not look at the things which are seen, but at the things which are not seen. For the things which are seen are temporary, but the things which are not seen are eternal"* (2 Corinthians 4:18). Thus I reasoned with myself: if I provide only for a prison, then the whip comes unawares, and so also the pillory. If I only provide for these, then I am not fit for banishment. Further, if I conclude that banishment is the worst, then if death comes I am surprised. Thus I see the best way to go through sufferings is to trust in

God through Christ, in regard to the world to come, and as touching this world, to count *"the grave as my house,...[to] make my bed in the darkness, and...[to] say to corruption, 'You are my father,' and to the worm, 'you are my mother and sister'"* (Job 17:14). That is to familiarize these things to me.

But notwithstanding these helps, I found myself a man encompassed with infirmities. The parting with my wife and poor children has often been to me in this place as pulling the flesh from the bones, not only because I am somewhat too fond of these great mercies, but also because I would have often brought to my mind the many hardships, miseries, and needs that my poor family were likely to meet with should I be taken from them, especially my poor blind child, who lay nearer to my heart than all the others. Oh, the thoughts of the hardship my poor blind one might undergo would break my heart to pieces. Poor child, what sorrow are you likely to have for your portion in this world! You must be beaten, must beg, suffer hunger, cold, nakedness, and a thousand calamities, though I cannot now endure that the wind should blow upon you. Yet, recalling myself, I thought that I must entrust you all with God, though it goes to the quick to leave you. Oh, I saw in this condition I was as a man who was pulling down his house upon the head of his wife and children. "Yet," thought I, "I must do it, I must do it." And now I thought on those two milk cows that were to carry the ark of God into another country, and to leave their calves behind them (1 Samuel 6:10).

But what helped me in this temptation were diverse considerations, of which, three especially here I will name. The first was the considerations of these two Scriptures: *"Leave your fatherless children, I will preserve them alive; and let your widows trust in Me"* (Jeremiah 49:11), and again, *"The Lord said, Surely it will be well with your remnant; surely I will cause the enemy to intercede with you in the time of adversity and in the time of affliction"* (Jeremiah 15:11).

I had also this consideration, that if I should venture all for God, I engaged God to take care of my concerns. However, if I forsook Him in His ways for fear of any trouble that should come to me or mine, then I would not only falsify my profession, but should count also that my concerns

were not so sure if left at God's feet while
I stood to and for His name, as they would
be if they were under my own care, though
with the denial of the way of God. This was
a smarting consideration, and spurred into
my flesh. That Scripture in which Christ
prays that God would disappoint Judas in
his selfish thoughts which moved him to
sell his Master, also greatly helped the
sting to fasten the more on me. Pray read
Psalm 109 soberly.

I had also another consideration: that
walk—the dread of the torments of hell—
of which I was sure they must partake who
do shrink from their profession of Christ,
His words, and laws before the sons of men
for fear of the cross. I thought also of the
glory that He had prepared for those that
in faith and love and patience stood to His
ways before men. These things, I say, have
helped me when the thoughts of the misery
that both myself and mine might, for the
sake of my profession, be exposed to, have
pinched at my mind.

When I have indeed conceded that I
might be banished for my profession, then
I have thought of that Scripture: *"They
were stoned, they were sawn in two, were
tempted, were slain with the sword. They*

wandered about in sheep skins and goat skins, being destitute, afflicted, tormented, of whom the world was not worthy" (Hebrews 11:37-38). For all that, they thought they were too bad to dwell and abide among them. I have also thought of that saying, *"The Holy Spirit testifies in every city, saying that chains and afflictions await me"* (Acts 20:23). I have truly thought that in my soul I have sometimes reasoned about the sore and sad estate of a banished and exiled condition: how those in exile are exposed to hunger, to cold, to perils, to nakedness, to enemies, and a thousand calamities, and at last perhaps to die in a ditch like a poor and desolate sheep. But I thank God, hitherto I have not been moved by these most delicate reasonings, but have rather by them more approved my heart to God.

I was once, above all the rest, in a very sad and low condition for many weeks. At that time also, being but a young prisoner and not acquainted with the laws, I had this lying upon my spirits, that my imprisonment might end at the gallows, for all that I could tell. Now, therefore, Satan laid hard at me to beat me out of heart by suggesting unto me: "But what if, when you come indeed to die, you should be in this condition, not savoring the things of God, nor having an evidence upon your soul for a better state hereafter?" For indeed at this time all the things of God were hidden from my soul. Thus, when I at first began to think of this, it was a great trouble to me, for I thought to myself that in the condition I now was in I was not fit to die. Neither did I think I could if I should be called to it. Besides, I thought to myself that if I should make a scrambling shift to clamber up the ladder, yet I should, either with quaking or other symptoms of fainting, give occasion to the enemy to reproach the way of God and His people for their timorousness.

This therefore lay with great trouble upon me, for I thought I was ashamed to die with a pale face and tottering knees in such a case as this. Wherefore I prayed to God that He would comfort me and give me strength to do and suffer what He should call me to. Yet no comfort appeared, but all continued hidden. I was also at this time so really possessed with the thought of death, that often it was as if I was on the ladder with a rope about my neck. Only this was some encouragement to me: I thought I

might now have an opportunity to speak
my last words unto a multitude which I
thought would come to see me die. And I
thought if it must be so, if God will but
convert one soul by my last words, I shall
not count my life thrown away or lost. But
yet all the things of God were kept out of
my sight, and still the tempter followed me
with, "But where must you go when you
die? What will become of you? Where will
you be found in another world? What evidence have you for heaven and glory and
an inheritance among them that are sanctified?" Thus I was tossed about for many
weeks and knew not what to do. At last
this consideration fell with weight upon
me: that it was for the Word and way of
God that I was in this condition. Therefore
I was engaged not to flinch a hair's breadth
from it.

I thought also that God might choose
whether He would give me comfort now or
at the hour of death, but I might not therefore choose whether I would hold my profession or not. I was bound, but He was
free. Yes, it was my duty to stand upon His
Word, whether He would ever look upon
me or save me at the last. Wherefore I
reasoned, "Save the point being thus, I am

for going on and risking my eternal state with Christ, whether I have comfort here or not. If God does not come in," thought I, "I will leap off the ladder even blindfolded into eternity, sink or swim, come heaven, come hell. Lord Jesus, if You will catch me, do; if not, I will venture all for Your name."

I was no sooner fixed in this resolution, but this word dropped in my spirit: *"Does Job fear God for nothing?"* (Job 1:9), as if the accuser had said, "Lord, Job is no upright man: he serves You for respect of conditions." *"Have You not made a hedge about him?"* *"But now stretch out Your hand and touch all that he has, and he will surely curse You to Your face"* (Job 1:10-11).

I thought, "Is this the sign of an upright soul, to desire to serve God when all is taken from him? Is he a godly man that will serve God for nothing, rather than give up? Blessed be God, then I hope I have an upright heart, for I am resolved, God giving me strength, never to deny my profession of faith, though I have nothing at all for my pains."

As I was thus considering, Psalm 44:12-26 was set before me. Now was my heart full of comfort, for I hoped it was sincere. I would not have been without this trial for much. I am comforted every time I think of it, and I hope I shall bless God forever for the teachings I have had by it. Many more of the dealings of God toward me I might relate, but these, from the spoils won in battle, have I dedicated for the maintainance of the house of the Lord (1 Chronicles 26:27).

Conclusions

Of all the temptations that I ever met with in my life, to question the being of God and the truth of His Gospel is the worst, and the worst to bear. When this temptation comes, it takes away my girdle from me, and removes the foundation from under me. Oh, I have often thought of that word, *"having girded your waist with truth"* (Ephesians 6:14), and of that, *"If the foundations are destroyed, what can the righteous do?"* (Psalm 11:3).

Sometimes after having committed sin, when I have looked for sore chastisement from the hand of God, the very next that I have had from Him has been the discovery of His grace. Sometimes, when I have been comforted, I have called myself a fool for my so sinking under trouble. Then again, when I have been cast down, I thought I was not wise to give such way to comfort. With such strength and weight have both these been upon me.

I have wondered much at this one thing: that although God does visit my soul with ever so blessed a discovery of Himself, yet I have found that such hours have attended me afterwards, that I have been in my spirit so filled with darkness that I could not so much as once conceive of what that God and that comfort was with which I have been refreshed.

I have sometimes seen more in a line of the Bible than I could well tell how to stand and walk therein. Yet at other times the whole Bible has been to me as a dry stick, or rather, my heart has been so dead and dry unto it that I could not conceive the least dram of refreshment, though I have looked it all over.

Of all fears, the best are those that are made by the blood of Christ. Of all joy, the sweetest is that mixed with mourning over Christ. Oh, it is a good thing to be on our knees, with Christ in our arms, before God. I hope I know something of these things.

I find to this day seven abominations in my heart:

1. An inclining to unbelief,
2. Suddenly to forget the love and mercy that Christ manifests,

3. A leaning to the works of the law,

4. Wanderings and coldness in prayer,

5. To forget to watch for what I pray for,

6. Aptness to murmur because I have no more, and yet ready to abuse what I have, and

7. I can do none of those things which God commands me without my corruptions thrusting themselves in. *"I find then a law, that evil is present with me, the one who wills to do good"* (Romans 7:21).

These things I continually see and feel, and am afflicted and oppressed with, yet the wisdom of God does order them for my good:

1. They make me abhor myself;

2. They keep me from trusting my heart;

3. They convince me of the insufficiency of all inherent righteousness;

4. They show me the necessity of flying to Jesus;

5. They press me to pray unto God;
6. They show me the need I have to watch and be sober; and
7. They provoke me to pray unto God, through Christ, to help me and carry me through the world.

Addendum

The Reverend Robert Philip, author of *Bunyan's Life and Times,* adds the following:

Bunyan's liberation from prison was obtained from Charles II by Whitehead the Quaker. On his release he soon became one of the most popular preachers of the day and was, if not the chaplain, "the teacher" of Sir John Shorter, the Mayor of London.

But although free and popular, Bunyan evidently dreaded every new crisis in public affairs. He had reason to do so. Venner's conspiracy had increased the severity of his first six years' imprisonment. On the occasion of the fire in London, he was thrown into prison again. And soon after James II came to the throne in 1685, Bunyan conveyed the whole of his property to his wife by a singular deed, which can only be accounted for by his suspicions of James and Jeffries, and by his horror at the revocation of the Edict of Nantz. The asylum which the refugees found in England did not prove to him that he was safe. No wonder. Kirke and "his lambs" were abroad and the Bedford justices still in power. It was under these circumstances that he divested himself of all his property, in order to save his family from want should he again be made a victim. The deed shows his solicitude for Mrs. Bunyan's comfort and his confidence in her prudence. And his Elizabeth well deserved both.

Whatever Bunyan may have feared when he thus disposed of all the little property he had, nothing befell him under James II. He published *The Pharisee and Publican* in 1685, the year of the king's accession.

In 1688, Charles Doe says, "He published six books, being the time of King James II's liberty of conscience." This appears from Doe's list. It throws also much light upon Bunyan's death. Such labor could not fail to sap his strength, even if he did nothing but carry the six books to the press, for none of them are small except the last. "He was seized with a sweating distemper," says Doe, "after he published six books, which, after some weeks, proved his death."

The sketch in the British Museum states that, "taking a tedious journey in a slabbing rainy day, and returning late to London, he was entertained by one Mr. Strudwick, a grocer on Snow Hill, with all the kind endearments of a loving friend, but soon found himself indisposed with a kind of shaking, as it were an ague, which increasing to a fever, he took to his bed, where, growing worse, he found he had not long to last in this world, and therefore prepared himself for another, towards which he had been journeying as a pilgrim and stranger upon earth the prime of his days."

The occasion of his journey to Reading, which has always been called "a labor of love and charity," will now be more interesting than it hitherto has been. It was not undertaken by a man in health, but by an overwrought author sinking with "a sweating distemper." Mr. Ivimey's account of Bunyan's errand being the best, I quote it:

The last act of his life was a labor of love and charity. A young gentleman, a neighbor of Mr. Bunyan, falling under his father's displeasure, and being much troubled in mind on that account, and also from hearing it was his father's design to disinherit him, or otherwise deprive him of what he had to leave, he pitched upon Mr. Bunyan as a fit man to make way for his submission, and prepare his mind to receive him; which he, being willing to undertake any good office, readily engaged in, and went to Reading, in Bedfordshire, for that purpose. There he so successfully accomplished his design, by using such pressing arguments and reason against anger and passion, and also for love and reconciliation, that the father's heart was softened, and his bowels yearned over his son.

After Mr Bunyan had disposed of everything in the best manner to promote an accommodation, as he returned to London on horseback, he was overtaken with excessive rains, and coming to his lodgings extremely wet, he fell sick of a violent fever, which he bore with much constancy and patience, and expressed himself as if he wished nothing more than to depart and to be with Christ, considering it as gain, and life only a tedious delay of expected felicity. Finding his strength decaying, he settled his worldly affairs as well as the shortness the time and the violence of the disorder would permit; and after an illness of ten days, with unshaken confidence he resigned his soul, on the 31st of August, 1688, being sixty years of age, into the hand of his most merciful Redeemer, following his Pilgrimage from the city of Destruction to the New Jerusalem, his better part having been all along there in holy contemplation, panting, and breathing after the hidden manna and the water of life.

His tomb is in Bunhill Fields. His cottage at Elstow, although somewhat modernized, is substantially as he left it. His chair, jug, *Book of Martyrs*, church book, and some other relics are carefully preserved at his chapel in Bedford. And best of all, his catholic spirit also is preserved there.